S0-AHI-212

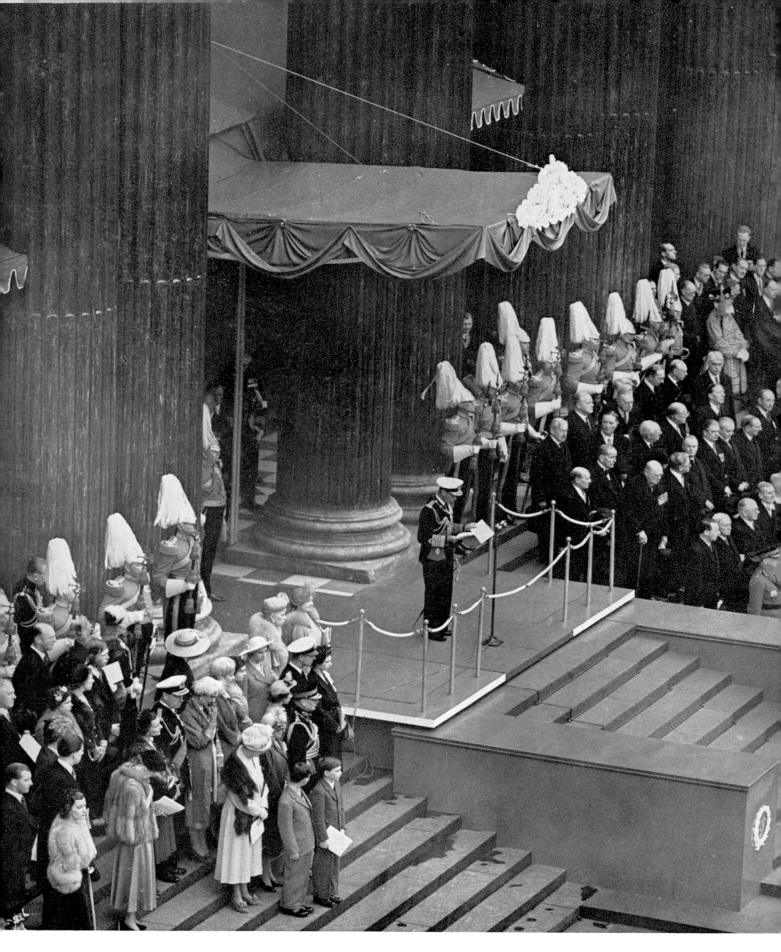

H.M. the King opens the Festival of Britain from the steps of St. Paul's Cathedral.

ROYAL ALBUM

EDITED BY
H. TATLOCK MILLER

DESIGNED & DECORATED BY
LOUDON SAINTHILL

THE HOUSE OF HUTCHINSON
LONDON
1951

First Published 1951

Some of the photographs in this book
are copyright reserved and may not be
reproduced without written permission

MADE AND PRINTED IN GREAT BRITAIN
BY THE HUTCHINSON PRINTING TRUST, LTD.

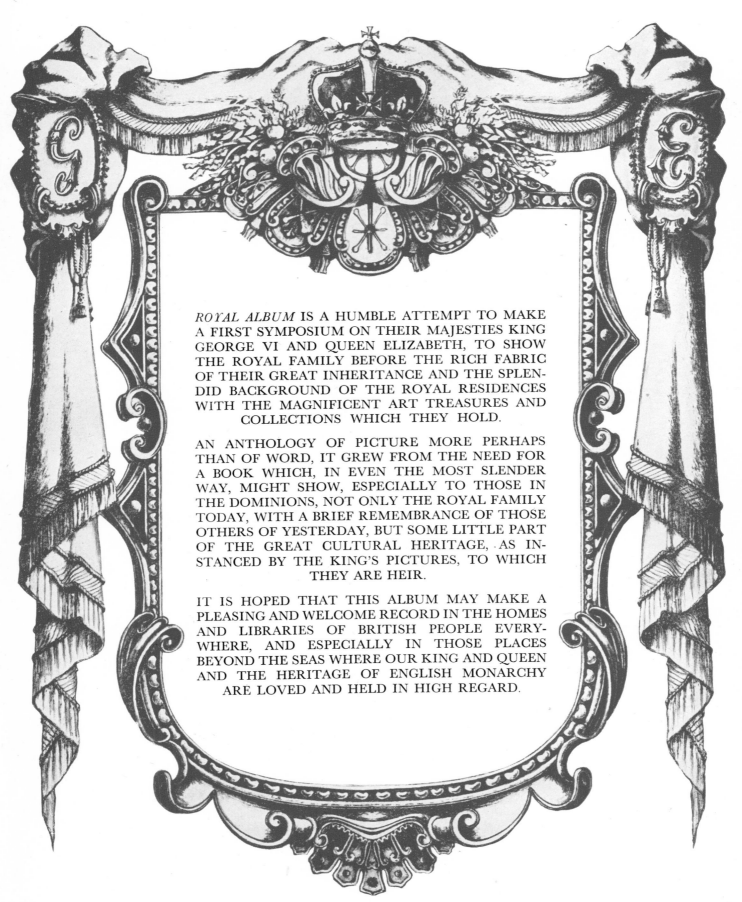

ROYAL ALBUM IS A HUMBLE ATTEMPT TO MAKE A FIRST SYMPOSIUM ON THEIR MAJESTIES KING GEORGE VI AND QUEEN ELIZABETH, TO SHOW THE ROYAL FAMILY BEFORE THE RICH FABRIC OF THEIR GREAT INHERITANCE AND THE SPLENDID BACKGROUND OF THE ROYAL RESIDENCES WITH THE MAGNIFICENT ART TREASURES AND COLLECTIONS WHICH THEY HOLD.

AN ANTHOLOGY OF PICTURE MORE PERHAPS THAN OF WORD, IT GREW FROM THE NEED FOR A BOOK WHICH, IN EVEN THE MOST SLENDER WAY, MIGHT SHOW, ESPECIALLY TO THOSE IN THE DOMINIONS, NOT ONLY THE ROYAL FAMILY TODAY, WITH A BRIEF REMEMBRANCE OF THOSE OTHERS OF YESTERDAY, BUT SOME LITTLE PART OF THE GREAT CULTURAL HERITAGE, AS INSTANCED BY THE KING'S PICTURES, TO WHICH THEY ARE HEIR.

IT IS HOPED THAT THIS ALBUM MAY MAKE A PLEASING AND WELCOME RECORD IN THE HOMES AND LIBRARIES OF BRITISH PEOPLE EVERYWHERE, AND ESPECIALLY IN THOSE PLACES BEYOND THE SEAS WHERE OUR KING AND QUEEN AND THE HERITAGE OF ENGLISH MONARCHY ARE LOVED AND HELD IN HIGH REGARD.

ACKNOWLEDGMENTS

IN the course of compiling a book of this nature too many debts of gratitude are incurred for it to be possible to enumerate them; but humble thanks are offered, and grateful acknowledgment made, to those who have made this Album possible.

Special acknowledgment must be made to The Controller of H.M. Stationery Office, H.M. Office of Works, the British Museum, the National Gallery, the Victoria and Albert Museum, the British Council, the Arts Council of Great Britain, the Kensington Public Library, the Westminster City Council, the Central Office of Information, the Royal College of Arms, and to the Marquis of Carisbrooke, G.C.B., the Earl and Countess of Gowrie, Sir Owen F. Morshead, K.C.V.O., Sir Shuldham Redfern, Rex de C. Nan Kivell, Esq., the Earl Amherst, M.C., Mrs. William Searle, Alec Murray, Esq., Charles Wilmot, Esq., Roi de Mestre, Esq., Mrs. H. V. Hodson, Colonel M. Sandford, Terence Wright, Esq., Edgar Ritchard, Esq., Collie Knox, Esq., Miss Antonia Blaxland, Mrs. Max Parrish, Frank Maggs, Esq., G. H. Chettle, Esq., F.S.A., H. E. Bates, Esq., Miss Sophie Fedorovitch, F. A. Mercer, Esq., Miss K. Frost, John Overton, Esq., Miss Anne Matheson, Hedley Jeffries, Esq., C. H. Gibbs-Smith, Esq., J. F. Physick, Esq., Peter Lubbock, Esq., Julian Frisby, Esq., Executors of the late Sydney Ure Smith, D. D. O'Connor, Esq., Mrs. Gregory Blaxland, Alfred Hecht, Esq., Miss Jocelyn Rickards, David Wild, Esq., Professor A. J. Ayer, Miss Fiona Smith.

Acknowledgment is also made to the Editor, *Art et Style*, and the Editor, *The Studio*, for several of the colour plates, and *Country Life*, Picture Post Library, the Associated Press, Ltd., Dorothy Wilding, Hay Wrightson, F.R.S.A., Helmut Gernsheim, F.R.P.S., Karsh, of Ottawa, Camera Press, Ltd., The Topical Press, Ltd., Barratts, Ltd., Studio Lisa, Sport & General, Keystone Press, Ltd., Fox, Ltd., and to Marcus Adams.

CONTENTS

COLOUR PLATES

ERRATA

Page 34 The date of the Coronation should be 1937.

Page 68 The caption "The Throne Room" should appear beneath the right-hand picture and "The White Drawing-room" beneath the left.

Page 185 Centre top caption. For Prince Michael read Prince Edward.

HIS MOST EXCELLENT MAJESTY

GEORGE VI

BY THE GRACE OF GOD,
OF GREAT BRITAIN,
IRELAND, AND OF
THE BRITISH DOMINIONS
BEYOND THE SEAS,
KING, DEFENDER OF THE FAITH

Karsh

HER MAJESTY

QUEEN ELIZABETH

Cecil Beaton

Hay Wrightson, F.R.P.S.

HER MAJESTY QUEEN MARY

THE
ROYAL FAMILY

ARTHUR BRYANT

FOR FIFTEEN YEARS, including some of the most troubled and perilous, as well as most glorious, in British history, King George VI and his consort, Queen Elizabeth, have reigned over the British Empire, now called the Commonwealth of Nations, occupying the historic thrones of England and Scotland on which the King's ancestors have sat for nearly a thousand years. They have embodied their people's aspirations, shared their perils, griefs and achievements and rejoiced with them in times of national gladness. And their subjects, identifying the King and Queen with the corporate existence of their commonwealth, have followed the domestic and personal lives of their Sovereigns, with an interest, affection and pride that men and women usually reserve for members of their own family. For the well-being, happiness and personal stability of the King and Queen are (in a symbolic sense) guarantees for the well-being, happiness and personal stability, not of any particular British family, but of millions of British families now living, and others whose life is still to be lived, throughout the world.

The British Empire, it has been said, is a family affair, and the Royal house in more than one sense symbolises it; the family is the unit which feeds and maintains that Empire and for which in the final resort it exists. Family life, though the source of the truest and most enduring happiness that can come to most men and women in this troubled world, is contrary to some of the strongest and most selfish instincts that tyrannise over the human heart. It necessitates continued and habitual self-sacrifice, the stifling of fancy, the renunciation of pleasures and liberties that tempt the heart of man—and woman, too. It does not, therefore, arise naturally and, generally when practised, depends, at least in part, on the imaginative force of an ideal and a widely recognised moral social belief and on example. Such an example, founded on the Christian faith and the proved practice and morality of centuries, the King and Queen are expected to afford their subjects by their own married life and the wise upbringing of their children. If they should fail to do so, even the most fanatic republican would admit that the institution of marriage throughout the Empire would be weakened and that many who, given that visible example from the Throne, might have restrained dangerous impulses and so helped to ensure the success of their married lives and their children's upbringing, would have one incentive less to show restraint and care. Every successful marriage tends to create others, and every unsuccessful marriage, by however little, to undermine others. And if this be true of the marriages of ordinary men and women in private station, how much more true must it be of the marriages of kings and queens and, still more so, of a King and Queen reigning over nearly a quarter of the globe.

This helps to explain the instinct which causes millions of men and women who have never set eyes on the King and Queen to follow their private life with interest and to rejoice at its joys and triumphs. It is, in the sphere of matters politic, the same instinct that renders popular those never-ending and apparently uneventful dramas of everyday and happy family life in which the B.B.C., interpreting a deep psychological need, affords to ordinary men and women and their sons and daughters, a chance to dramatise their own struggles to live together happily and, by dramatizing them, to render them successful. Such dramas make the real and, indeed, supreme importance of such struggles clear, and that, after all, is a considerable service to mankind, however little it may appeal to those absorbed in the pursuit of intellectual abstractions. In the case of the Throne, such a dramatisation of the virtues of family life serves a civic end whose value it is almost impossible to exaggerate. The personal responsibility resting on the shoulders of a King and Queen whose everyday actions are the subject of interest, conversation and speculation in forty or fifty countries scattered around the globe is no trivial matter. It is an essential part, and a very important one, of the many services we expect from the fellow human beings who happen to occupy the throne. We are right to rejoice and to pay them honour when they so manifestly and triumphantly succeed in it.

The Crown exists primarily to help afford to an organised society two things of which it particularly stands in need: stability and continuance. As individuals men possess pathetic-ally little of either: it is only when they associate as members of a social organisation that they, in some measure, acquire them. The family is the first social organism that offers us a means to these: the State, rightly viewed, is only a wider social organism, made up of many families, to give them the strength of mutual support and so ensure their capacity for affording stability and continuance. The Royal family is the outward and visible sign of this inward and visible truth. It stands firm and it continues from age to age. The preservation of stability is a function of the Crown which is more than ordinarily valuable —indeed, priceless—in a revolutionary age. The more important and essential the revolu-tion, the truer this becomes. For by preserving stability at such a time the Crown can not only save the ordinary man and woman from the unspeakable sufferings which befall them when revolution temporarily results in the collapse of social order and the emergence of the rule of violence, but, by avoiding the moral degeneration and inevitable reaction which such violence always brings in its train, it paradoxically facilitates and even speeds the course of necessary revolution. This is where our constitutional monarchy has proved of such inestimable value. For instead of acting as a dam to revolutionary currents—a dam, that is, to what may be inevitable and necessary—it serves as a salutary embankment to keep the onward stream in a true and steady course. In the nineteenth century, for instance, the existence of our constitutional monarchy and the people's respect and affection for it enabled the great and necessary social changes which the leaders of the French Revolution had proclaimed, to take place in this country—so far as practical and real results were concerned—far more rapidly than they did in France. In France there was an untrammelled revolution repeatedly and inevitably followed by reaction: in the years 1789–1815, in 1830, in 1848, in 1871. In England, except so far as it was caused by the wars which French revolutionary lawlessness and international violence and aggression had

Cecil Beaton

HIS MAJESTY KING GEORGE VI

HER MAJESTY QUEEN ELIZABETH

imposed on her, there was no reaction. There was merely steady and unbroken progress based on the very truths and needs which the French Revolution had emphasised and made vocal. In the great reforms of 1827, 1832 and 1835, of the Peelite 'forties and the Gladstonian 'sixties, monarchical Britain far outdistanced republican France in the practical application of liberal principles. The enduring monarchy of George III's descendants saw long before any other European country the realisation of the dreams of Rousseau and Tom Paine. This, I feel, has never been sufficiently appreciated.

Exactly the same thing has happened in our own time. Since 1923, the year when the Duke of York, as he then was, married the daughter of the Earl of Strathmore, Britain has experienced a social, economic and political revolution of the first magnitude, yet has done so without either bloodshed or reaction. At that time the wage of an agricultural worker was just over thirty shillings a week, mass unemployment was regarded as the proper and only way of checking an inflationary situation, and the idea of a Labour Government in Britain was still unthinkable to many people and associated in the popular mind with the tumbril and red republicanism. I remember how, a decade or so earlier, my father's table was strewn every morning with obscure Labour newspapers which, in the course of his official duties he used to study in order to keep abreast with republican and similar trends. They did not, perhaps, require very much study, for those trends shouted at one from every flamboyant headline. Every issue of every journal—and they were legion, though mostly of minute circulation—bore pictures of a bloated and fiendlike capitalist, with top-hat, distended waistcoat and enormous golden watch-chain, sucking the blood or otherwise maltreating a famished, emaciated and tortured-looking working-man or family. As for crowns and coronets, they were symbols, according to these papers, of everything hypocritical, vile and reactionary—a kind of base cloak for capitalist practices and deserving the contempt and hatred of every honest working-man. Their language, indeed, was not unlike that of the Press of the remoter and redder Balkan Republics at the present time. If the kind of men who wrote and read them, the reader felt, should ever attain political power, most of those in present authority would perish on the gallows or swing from a lamp-post.

Yet when they attained that power nothing of the kind happened. Most of the British revolutionary prophets of the early years of the century have not only since held high and honourable office under the Crown, but in many cases have become members of an hereditary House of Lords and staunch upholders of the monarchical principle. This is not because they have changed their basic aims—justice and the amelioration of the worker's lot—but because they have realised that those aims are not only attainable within the existing monarchical framework of the country, but can be attained far more surely and speedily within it than without, and with far less interference with the day-by-day happiness of those whom such reforms are intended to benefit. In that realisation—one that has probably saved Britain not only from revolution and civil war, but from such a division and collapse in the face of foreign aggression as befell a far less industrialised democratic neighbour in 1940—the Monarchy has played a most important part. For King George V and Queen Mary, King Edward VIII during his brief reign and still more during his long and arduous years of national service as Prince of Wales, and the present King and Queen have all consistently striven to bridge the social gap brought about by the abuses of the Industrial Revolution. For the past quarter of a century and more the members of the Royal family have again and again gone out of their way to make it clear that they were at the service of all their subjects, irrespective of wealth, class or political opinion. This cannot always have been easy, for princes, like other men, are in part the creatures of their environment and upbringing and the outlook and prejudices which these inevitably create. They find criticism, particularly unfair criticism, no easier to bear than anyone else. Yet the Crown has indisputably been held high above all party strife and class feeling, and its impartiality has been recognised as clearly by the unprivileged as by the privileged. Thanks to its wearers, the Crown has been as much the common property of all British men and women as Westminster Abbey or the cliffs of Dover. It has been common property not only in respect of birth and station, but in respect of space. King George VI and Queen Elizabeth belong just as much to the New Zealand sheep-farmer and the Canadian miner as they do to Cockney clerks whose office windows in Grosvenor Place look over the Palace gardens. And they belong, equally, to the Fiji islanders and the tribesmen of equatorial Africa. That is a very remarkable fact.

How well they have fulfilled their historic trust can be seen by looking back over the revolutionary events of the past twenty-five years. When the King and Queen were married, Great Britain did not seem a very stable place: there was bitter class feeling, grave industrial unrest and widespread talk of revolutionary action. Three years later came the General Strike of 1926: the nearest England had come to civil war for a century. But the country proved too united to be broken on those deeply-felt divisions, and it was, in no small measure, the binding influence of the Crown which kept Englishmen from fighting Englishmen.

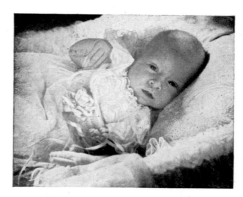

Above: H.R.H. Princess Elizabeth. The first photographs of H.R.H. Prince Charles of Edinburgh (above right), and (below) H.R.H. Princess Anne

H.R.H. Princess Elizabeth

Cecil Beaton

Thereafter, with Labour's coming-of-age and the long conciliatory political reign of Stanley Baldwin, class feeling in Britain began to grow not more, but less, intense, and this despite the terrible and blighting evil of mass unemployment which first gripped the country in the year before the Royal marriage. The lessening of hatred between class and class and the growing sense of the oneness of a Britain so long divided into Disraeli's "two nations" was probably due as much to King George V's and Queen Mary's dignity, sense of duty and understanding of their countrymen as to any other single factor. In their great work they were nobly assisted by the Duke of York and his charming young Duchess—the spiritual heirs to those unifying qualities. One contribution to that work made at that stage in his career by the present King was the Duke of York's annual holiday camp when boys, drawn in equal numbers from the public schools and the factories, met in happy and fruitful companionship under the personal leadership of the man who was to be their future King. It was only, of course, a symbol—one little island of example in the great ocean of social unrest and suspicion. Yet, with the impress of the Crown set upon it, it was one which had consequences whose extent it is difficult to assess. It made clear to all the spirit of comrade-ship which has always been the British ideal and which alone can solve Britain's difficulties, and to which we turned, as to a light in a storm, in 1940, and to which we must turn again today if we are to be saved. Of the great liberal and revolutionary triune—liberty, equality, fraternity—liberty has been, *in excelsis*, the ideal of the great American Republic, equality that of the French Republic, fraternity that of the free and constitutional British monarchy. And in moments of crisis a nation always goes back to its roots.

The Christening of Princess Anne Elizabeth Alice Louise

Her Royal Highness Princess Margaret   *Cecil Beaton*

Two things, above all, every Briton living today owes to the Throne and to the King and Queen. That a "cold" Revolution through which we have passed, and are still passing, has remained a "cold" and not a "hot" revolution, and that the nations of the British Commonwealth, in the face of every separatist tendency and under overwhelming stress, have drawn not farther apart, but closer together. The full extent of that revolution may have been obscured by the mildness of its methods, but it has been a tremendous revolution none the less. To realise it one has only to think of the incredibly changed circumstances of tens of thousands now living who were born into a world of wealth, security, status and personal power and liberty which has today utterly vanished for them. The England of the upper and upper-middle class of King Edward VII's reign is almost as unlike our own age as that of the eighteenth century or the days of Queen Elizabeth. Those whose impressions have been formed in it are living in a world which seems to them alien and strangely naked; but they are living and contributing their own quota—a very great one—of historic tradition, culture and public service to the new England they have seen born around them. There has been no guillotine and the victims of revolution have passed forward in the tumbril with dignity and good humour into the revolutionaries' promised land, and have there—though with many sad and nostalgic memories of a, for them, happier world—set to work like pioneers to lay the foundations of a new civilisation for the many which may one day equal in liberty, beauty and dignity the civilisation for the few of which they were the happy inheritors. And the many have entered into their promised land of greater opportunity —sadly shorn though it may be by the destruction of two terrible wars—without a trace of the fearful upheavals and social sufferings that have marred the lives of the first generation of the beneficiaries of all other national revolutions. That happiness they owe, in my belief, more to the Crown than to any other institution.

So, too, with the Empire—not only our salvation in war but, though we may not yet realise it, our economic life-line along which we can alone hope to escape the consequences of our unbalanced island trade and population. It has not been our democratic Parliament in Westminster, great though that is, but our constitutional Crown which has proved the spiritual centre of that mighty union of British hearts and minds throughout the world. It would not have done so had not those who were called upon to wear it proved worthy in themselves of the world-wide love and trust it inspires.

The Christening of Princess Anne

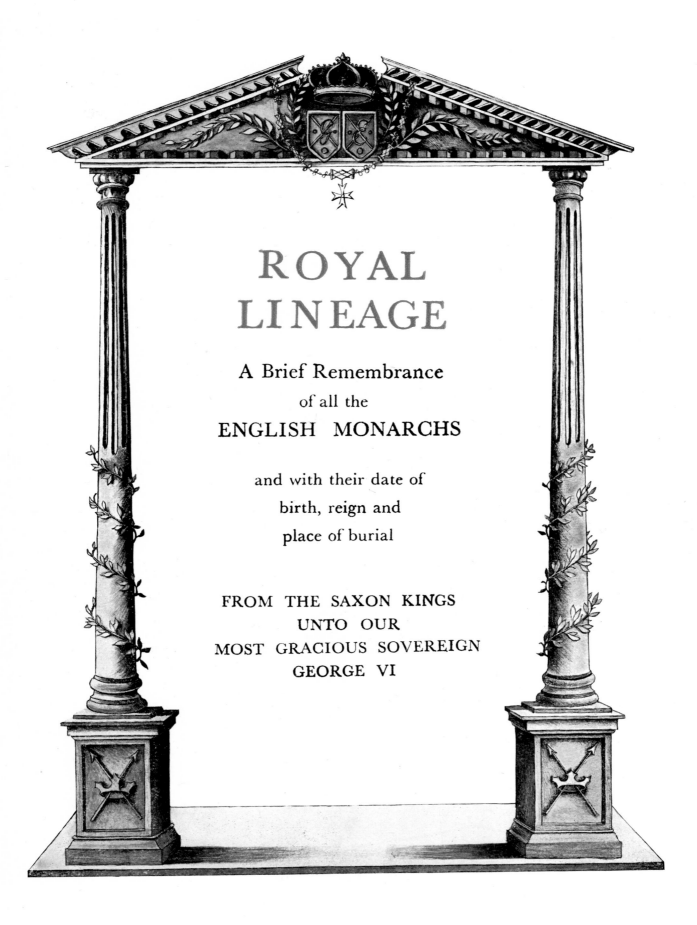

ROYAL LINEAGE

A Brief Remembrance
of all the
ENGLISH MONARCHS

and with their date of
birth, reign and
place of burial

FROM THE SAXON KINGS
UNTO OUR
MOST GRACIOUS SOVEREIGN
GEORGE VI

EGBERT,

KING of the WEST SAXONS,

First Monarch of all ENGLAND.

THE SAXON KINGS

ETHELWOLF

Egbert's eldest son, succeeded him in 836, took a journey to Rome in 855, and paid 300 marks tribute yearly to the Pope. He died in 857 after having divided his kingdom between his two eldest sons, Ethelbald and Ethelbert

EDRED

Sixth son of Edward, succeeded his brother Edmund in 946, and was the first who was styled King of Great Britain. He died of a lingering distemper in the 10th year of his reign and was buried at Westminster

EDGAR

Brother of Edwin, succeeded him in 959, being sixteen years of age. He increased the Royal Navy to 3,600 ships, erected 47 monasteries, and reigned in greater splendour than any of his predecessors. He died in the 17th year of his reign, aged 32. Buried at Glastonbury

EGBERT. Reigned 10 years, descended from Cerdic, King of Wessex, a Saxon general who arrived in Britain in 495. Served under Charlemagne. Crowned King of Wessex in 800. Conquered Cornwall 813, Kent 819, Essex 823. Crowned King of England 827. Died 837. Married Lady Redburga

ETHELBALD. Reigned 3 years from 857

ETHELBERT. Reigned 6 years. King of all England on death of brother Ethelbald in 860

ETHELRED I. Reigned 5 years from 866

ALFRED. The Great. Reigned 29 years from 871. Crowned at Winchester 871. Married Ethelswitha. Introduced trial by jury, made London capital of England, translated Psalms and Aesop's Fables into Anglo-Saxon. Won 65 battles. Died at Oxford 901 and buried at Winchester

EDWARD I, the Elder. Reigned 24 years from 901. Born 872. Crowned at Kingston on Thames. Emperor of Britain 924. Founded University of Cambridge. Died at Farringdon, Berks, 925. Buried at Winchester

ATHELSTAN. Reigned 15 years from 925. Died 940 at Gloucester

EDMUND I. Reigned 6 years from 940. Born 923. Married Elgiva

EDWY. Reigned 4 years from 955. Married Elgiva. Died 959

SWEYN. Reigned 3 years from 1014. Drove Ethelred II into Normandy 1014, and on death of Sweyn in 1015 crown was continued by Edmund II and Canute

EDMUND II, the Ironside. Reigned 1 year from 1016. Born 989. Crowned at Kingston-on-Thames 1016 and died same year. Defeated by Canute and kingdom was divided between Canute and Edmund. At his death Canute was master of all England. The Danes were kings till 1041. Married Algitha

HAROLD I, the Harefoot. Reigned 3 years from 1036. Died 1039

HARDICANUTE. Reigned 2 years from 1039. Was also King of Denmark on Canute's death

EDWARD III, the Confessor. Reigned 25 years from 1041. Gained crown chiefly through Earl Godwin

HAROLD II. Reigned 1 year, 1066. Half-brother to Edward the Confessor

EDWARD
(The Martyr)

Eldest son to Edgar. Succeeded him when young in 975, and was murdered near Corfe Castle 978 by his stepmother, Queen Elfrida, to make room for her son, Ethelred. Buried at Shaftesbury

ETHELRED
(The Unready)

Half-brother to Edward, began his reign 979, and was crowned at Kingston. In 1012 Sweyn, King of Denmark, conquered England and Ethelred fled to Normandy. Recalled 1014. Died 1016, and was buried at St. Paul's

CANUTE
(The Great)

Upon the death of Edmund became King of all England in 1016. Divided England into four provinces, subdued Norway and was entitled King of England, Denmark, Norway and Sweden. Buried at Winchester 1036

THE HOUSE OF NORMANDY

WILLIAM THE FIRST, Duke of Normandy, surnamed the Conqueror. Son of Robert the Devil. Conquered the Saxon forces at Hastings and was crowned on Christmas Day, 1066, at Westminster. Reigned nearly 21 years, died in Normandy and buried there in 1087

WILLIAM THE SECOND, surnamed Rufus. Second son of the Conqueror. Was crowned at Westminster on Sunday, September 26th, 1087, being 21 years of age and reigned 12 years. Was killed by an arrow while hunting in the New Forest in August 1100. Buried at Winchester

HENRY THE FIRST, brother of William Rufus. Born at Selby in Yorkshire, crowned King on Sunday, August 5th, 1100, and reigned for 30 years. Married Matilda, daughter of Malcolm, King of Scotland. Invaded Normandy in 1106 and later conquered Wales. Died in the Forest of Lyons and buried in Reading Abbey, 1135

STEPHEN, grandson of William the Conqueror, crowned on Thursday, December 26th, 1135. Defeated the Scottish invasion in 1138, but his forces routed in battle led by Robert of Gloucester and his cousin Matilda. Died in 1154 and buried at Feversham

THE HOUSE OF PLANTAGENET

HENRY THE SECOND, Duke of Normandy, Guyen and Aquitaine. Crowned on Sunday, December 19th, 1154. Married Eleanor of Aquitaine. Buried in Normandy 1189

RICHARD THE FIRST, surnamed Cœur de Lion, son of Henry II, crowned Sunday, September 3rd, 1189, and led Third Crusade in 1190 with King of France. Died by a poisoned arrow 1199

JOHN, Duke of Normandy, Lord of Ireland, brother of Richard I, crowned Thursday, May 27th, 1199, and reigned 17 years. Signed Magna Carta 1214 and died 1216

HENRY THE THIRD, Duke of Normandy, son of John, crowned Friday, October 28th, 1216. Reigned 56 years. Married Eleanor of Provence. Died 1272 and buried at Westminster

EDWARD THE FIRST, eldest son of Henry III. Born at Westminster, and there crowned on Sunday, August 19th, 1272, and reigned 34 years. Died 1307, buried at Westminster

EDWARD THE SECOND, crowned at Westminster on Shrove Sunday, 1308. Married Isabella of France, and assassinated in barbarous fashion 1327 in Barkley Castle

EDWARD THE THIRD, King of England and France, born at Windsor 1313, crowned 1327. Defeated French at Crecy 1346. Died 1377 and lies buried at Westminster

RICHARD THE SECOND, born at Bordeaux (son of the Black Prince), crowned on Thursday, July 16th, 1377. He reigned 22 years, was deposed and died in 1399, and buried at Westminster

Henry II   Richard I   John   Henry III   Edward I   Edward II   Edward III   Richard I

THE HOUSE OF LANCASTER

HENRY THE FOURTH. Henry of Lancaster, first king born in England of English parents. Married as his second wife Joan of Navarre. Crowned on Tuesday, October 13th, 1399. Died while at his devotions in Westminster Abbey 1413

HENRY THE FIFTH, King of England and France. Crowned on Passion Sunday, April 9th, 1413. Defeated French at Agincourt. Died at Paris aged 35 years in 1422, and lies buried at Westminster

HENRY THE SIXTH began his reign at the age of eight months in 1422. Crowned at Westminster on Sunday, November 6th, 1429, and afterward crowned at Paris 1431. Married Margaret of Anjou, founded Eton and King's College. Died 1471

THE HOUSE OF YORK

EDWARD THE FOURTH. Crowned on Monday, June 29th, 1461, at the age of eighteen and reigned 22 years. Married Elizabeth Woodville. Died, after a life of luxury and self-indulgence, in 1483, and was buried at Windsor

EDWARD THE FIFTH, being 13 years of age, came to London in 1483, reigned two months, and was deposed of his crown by his unnatural uncle the Protector, Richard of Gloucester, and with his brother lost his life in the Tower, their burial unknown until rediscovered during reign of Charles II, and removed to Westminster 1674

RICHARD III, surnamed Crookback. Crowned king on Sunday, July 6th, 1483. Slain in battle on the field of Bosworth, near Leicester, in 1485. His crown retrieved and placed on the head of Henry of Richmond

ELIZABETH
Queene of ENGLAND,
France and Ireland,
Defender of the FAITH, &c.

ELIZABETH. The Virgin Queen, sister to Mary I. Began her reign on November 17th, 1558, and reigned for 44 years 4 months and 7 days. Died the 24th day of March, 1603, aged 69 years, and lies buried at Westminster

HENRY THE SEVENTH. Crowned on Sunday, October 30th, 1485, and reigned 25 years. Married Elizabeth, daughter of Edward IV. Died 1509, and lies buried at Westminster

HENRY THE EIGHTH. Was crowned king on Sunday, June 24th, 1509, reigned 38 years. He wedded Katherine of Aragon, Anne Boleyn, Jane Seymour, Ann of Cleves, Katherine Howard and Katherine Parr. Died 1547 and buried at Windsor

EDWARD THE SIXTH. Henry VIII's only son. Crowned on Sunday, February 20th, 1547, at the age of ten, already conversant in seven languages. Died of consumption in 1553. Buried at Westminster

MARY THE FIRST. Daughter of Henry VIII by his first wife, Katherine of Aragon. Began her reign of five years in 1553. Married Philip of Spain, and died racked by disease in 1558

THE HOUSE OF STUART

CHARLES THE FIRST

JAMES THE FIRST

JAMES THE FIRST, King James VI of Scotland, son of Queen Mary and great-great-grandson of Henry VII. Came to the English throne on the death of Elizabeth, and was crowned on Monday, July 25th, 1603. Reigned until his death in 1625. Buried at Westminster

CHARLES THE FIRST. Only surviving son of James I. Crowned king on Thursday, February 2nd, 1625. Married Henrietta of France. During great Civil War fled to Scotland, and on January 30th, 1649, was beheaded outside his own Palace of Whitehall, a dignified figure to the last

CHARLES THE SECOND. After the regime of Commonwealth, Charles II returned from exile in 1660, and was crowned in Scotland on January 1st, 1651. Married Catherine of Braganza. Died in 1685, and lies buried at Westminster

JAMES THE SECOND. Succeeded his brother, Charles II, in 1685. Married firstly Anne Hyde and, in 1687, Mary of Modena. Finally defeated by his son-in-law, William of Orange, at the Battle of the Boyne, 1690. Died 1701 and buried in Paris

CHARLES THE SECOND

JAMES THE SECOND

THE HOUSE OF ORANGE

WILLIAM THE THIRD of Nassau, Prince of Orange. Married in 1677 Mary, daughter of James II. Crowned with Queen Mary on April 11th, 1689

MARY THE SECOND. Wife of William III, who reigned jointly with him until her death in 1694

ANNE. Succeeded her brother-in-law, William III, and was crowned on St. George's Day, 1702. Reigned 12½ years until her death in 1714

THE HOUSE OF HANOVER

GEORGE I. Son of the Electress, Sophia of Hanover, a granddaughter of James I. Reigned 1714 until his death in a coach on the road to Osnabrück

GEORGE II. Succeeded his father and was crowned King on October 11th, 1727. He was married to Caroline of Anspach, and reigned until his death in 1760

GEORGE III, grandson of George II, whom he succeeded, was crowned with Queen Charlotte on September 22nd, 1761. Died blind and insane at Windsor in 1820

GEORGE IV. Son of George III. Married Caroline of Brunswick. Reigned 1820–30. Of extravagant tastes, he reconstructed Windsor Castle and built Brighton Pavilion

WILLIAM IV, Duke of Clarence. Third son of George III. Married Princess Adelaide of Saxe-Meiningen. Reigned 1830 until his death in 1837

VICTORIA, Queen of England. Ascended the throne in 1837 on the death of her uncle, William IV. Married her first cousin, Prince Albert of Saxe-Coburg and Gotha in 1841. Victoria, a beloved Queen, reigned 64 years and died at Osborne in 1901, aged 82

EDWARD THE SEVENTH. Son of Victoria and the Prince Consort. Married Alexandra, Princess of Denmark. Died 1910, having reigned for nine years

THE HOUSE OF WINDSOR

GEORGE THE FIFTH. Son of Edward VII and Queen Alexandra. Crowned King of England 1911. Married Princess Mary of Teck

EDWARD THE EIGHTH. Prince of Wales. Succeeded his father, George V, in 1936, but abdicated before his coronation in favour of his brother Albert, Duke of York

GEORGE VI was proclaimed King on the abdication of his brother Edward and crowned with his Queen, Elizabeth, on May the 12th, 1937

GEORGIUS II REX ET CAROLINA REGINA

Triumphal Arch Erected and Painted on the West end of Westminster Hall for the Coronation of his Maj.ty King George the Second and Queen Caroline.
October the 11.th 1727.

Dorothy Wilding

Their Majesties King George VI and Queen Elizabeth in Coronation Robes

Coronation Day, 1936.   The Royal Family

Coronation Day, 1911.
King George V and Queen Mary

The Royal Princesses at the
Coronation of George VI

The Coronation Procession
of George VI

The Coronation Procession of King Charles the Second, 1660

The Imperial Crown of State as worn
by George II for his Coronation in 1727

The Ceremony of the Peers' Homage to
His Majesty King George VI

Coronation, 1936. From left: the Princess Royal, the Duchess of Gloucester, the Duke
of Gloucester, Queen Mary, King George VI, Princess Margaret, Princess Elizabeth,
Queen Elizabeth, the Duke and Duchess of Kent and Princess Louise

Left: Queen Mary in Coronation robes, 1911. Right: The Coronation Procession of King James II, 1685

The Coronation of King Henry IV, 1367

The actual crowning of King George VI

Below : The Herbal Women at the Coronation of George IV led by Miss Fellowes, 1820

Queen Alexandra at the Coronation of Edward VII, 1901, attended by her pages, Viscount Torrington, the Marquis of Stafford, J. N. Bigge, Esquire, the Hon. Edward Lascelles, the Earl of Macclesfield and the Hon. Robert Palmer

Queen Alexandra at prayer in Coronation robes

The actual crowning of Queen Elizabeth

The invitation card to the Coronation of William IV and Queen Adelaide, 1851

Below : George IV at his Coronation, 1820, attended by nine Peers' sons

REGIA MAIESTAS

DIEV ET MON DROIT

ELIZABETH
1558–1603
Crowned Queen of England on Sunday, January 15th, 1558

The Coronation of George III in the Abbey of
Westminster, September 22nd, 1761

The Coronation Chair,
Westminster Abbey

Left: The Ampula and the Anointing Spoon. The oldest objects among the regalia, they are used in the solemn moment of coronation when the King's head, breast and palms are anointed with holy oil

Right : St. Edward's Crown or the Crown of England was made for Charles II and is used for the Coronation ceremony

Lower right: The Sceptre with the Cross signifies kingly power; is one of the most ancient of emblems used by the Roman emperors and Saxon kings

Bottom right : The Imperial Crown of State. Made for the coronation of Queen Victoria, it includes the great ruby given to the Black Prince in the 14th century which adorned the crown of Henry V at Agincourt

REGALIA

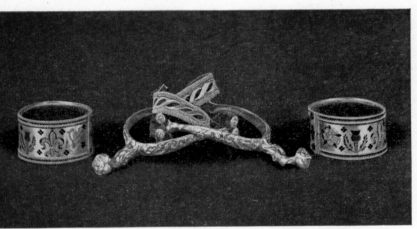

The Bracelets, of 17th century date, and the Golden Spurs, attributes of knighthood

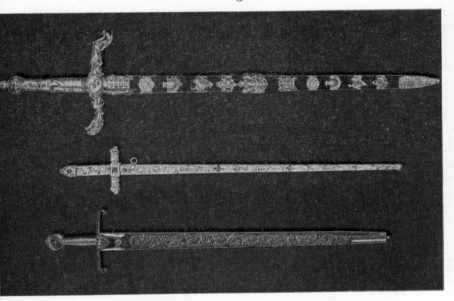

The Curtana, or Sword of Mercy, the jewelled Sword of State, made for the coronation of George IV, and the Great Sword of State, which represents the King's own personal sword

Their Majesties, George VI and Queen Elizabeth, in procession to the State Opening of Parliament in the Irish State Coach, October 1950

Henry Dymoke, the King's Champion at the Coronation of George IV

STATE COACH

The approach of the Monarch of Ocean is proclaimed by two Tritons blowing conch-shells on the front of the magnificent gilded State Coach. So important a part of Royal pageantry, pomp and circumstance, and drawn by eight Windsor greys, postilion-ridden it was built for George III to replace the State Coach of Queen Anne and has been used for Occasions of State since then. It cost £7,587 19s. 9½d. The panels are decorated with allegorical paintings by Cipriani, including the Royal Arms on the upper back panel, which is ornamented with the Order of St. George and the floral emblems of Great Britain. The carving is the work of Joseph Wilton. The details show the front of the Coach with its driver's footboard, formed of a large scallop shell ornamented with reeds, flanked by two Tritons blowing conch-shells and represented as drawing the Coach by means of cables. The decorated wheels are based on those of an ancient triumphal car. Harness is of red morocco leather

Queen Victoria and the Prince Consort

The marriage of Princess Anne, daughter of George II, to Prince William of Orange, 1734

ROYAL MARRIAGES

Left: The Royal Wedding of H.R.H. Princess Elizabeth and H.R.H. Prince Philip, the Duke of Edinburgh. Right: The Royal marriage licence of Princess Elizabeth and the Duke of Edinburgh

Left: The betrothal of King Charles the First to Henrietta of France, 1625
Centre: The marriage of Charles II, May 1662
Right: The betrothal of James I to Princess Anne, 1589

The wedding of the Duke and Duchess of York, 1923, attended by
the Earl and Countess of Strathmore, George V and Queen Mary

The drive to Parliament, 1932

The drive to the Guildhall, 1939

His Majesty King George the Sixth, at
the ceremony of Trooping the Colour

State opening of Parliament, 1938

OCCASIONS OF STATE

The Royal procession to the State Opening of Parliament

Homage to Their Majesties, King George V and Queen Mary,
at the Durbar, Delhi, 1912

On the balcony
of Shah Jehan's
Palace

THE DELHI DURBAR

The Royal procession at the Fort, Delhi

VISITS AND ANNIVERSARIES

Their Majesties with President Lebrun during the State Visit to Paris, 1938, and (right) the State Visit to Canada, 19

The Meeting of Henry VIII and Maximilian I (*by gracious permission of H.M. the King*)

The Royal Visit to the United States of America, 1939
The King drives with President Roosevelt

H.R.H. Princess Margaret at the Investiture o
Queen Juliana of Holland, Amsterdam, 194

Above (left and right): The Silver Jubilee and the Silver Wedding of Their Majesties George V and Queen Mary

Above left : H.R.H. the Duke of Gloucester during State Visit to Australia, 1934.   Centre : Queen Mary and H.M. Edward VIII arriving at the Cenotaph, Armistice Day, 1935.   Right : St. Paul's Cathedral Jubilee Thanksgiving Service of George V and Queen Mary, 1935

Left: The Royal Family at St. Paul's Cathedral for the Silver Jubilee Wedding Service, 1948.   Right: Their Majesties with the Princesses arriving to present Coronation Medals to Dominion and Colonial Troops, 1937

Members of the 10th Regiment of Light Dragoons.
From a painting in Windsor Castle by Stubbs

Left: Princess Mary,
Queen of Great Britain,
on horseback

Right: Coach presented
to Charles II by Count
Grammont, 1692

Princess Elizabeth and George VI
mounted at the ceremony of
Trooping the Colour

Above: King Henry VIII riding to a tournament
Right: King Charles II on horseback
Below: Victoria with John Brown, by Landseer

Left: George V as Colonel-in-Chief, Isle of Wight Rifles, 1897. Right: Royal
procession of Queen Elizabeth to visit the Right Hon. Henry Carey, Lord Hunsdon

Above: Command performance in honour of the State visit of the President of France, Royal Opera House, Covent Garden, 1939. The Royal Box was designed for the occasion by the late Rex Whistler

Right: Victoria and Albert at the Crystal Palace

Right: Royal Command Performance, London Coliseum, 1938

ROYAL COMMAND PERFORMANCES

Below: The Queen's retiring room at the Royal Opera House, Covent Garden, 1939

Below right: The Royal Fireworks exhibited on occasion of general peace, October 17th, 1748

Above: The Royal Family at the opening of the Great Exhibition in Hyde Park, May 1st, 1851. From a painting by Henry C. Selous

Left: H.R.H. the Duchess of Kent at the London Coliseum

Right: Their Majesties and Princess Margaret at a Royal Command film performance, Odeon Theatre, London

Below: H.M. Queen Elizabeth arriving at the French Embassy to dine with the President and Madame Lebrun, 1939

Queen Victoria and the Prince
Consort dancing the polka

Charles II dancing with his cousin, the Princess Palatine, in the Hague

Left:
Queen Victoria
at a banquet
given by the
London Corpora-
tion, 1837

Right:
Jeffrey Hudson,
dwarf enter-
tainer at the
Court of
Charles I

Below: The Royal party at the opening of Royal Ascot, June 19th, 1934

George V, Edward VII
and the Prince of Wales

H.M. the King in North
Africa, 1943, visiting units of
the U.S. and British fleets

Queen Mary and George V
on board S.S. *Medina* on
journey to India, 1912

H.R.H. the Duke of Edinburgh sails out to take
his first command, H.M.S. *Chequers*, Malta, 1950

Left: H.R.H. the Prince of Wales as a Bengal Lancer,
and (right) as he served in the First World War.
Below: H.M. George VI broadcasting to his
peoples throughout the world on Christmas Day

Her Gracious Majesty Elizabeth, Queen of England, on the
occasion of Her Majesty's fiftieth birthday. Portrait by Cecil Beaton

THE
KINGS
HOUSES

QUI
MAL Y PENSE
SOIT HONI

by HECTOR BOLITHO

Mars. Hampton Court Palace, the South Front designed by Sir Christopher Wren

Alec Murray

HAMPTON COURT PALACE

THE PRESENT KING once said, "I am not palace-minded": a remark that recalls an estimable but disappointing theme in the story of the Royal family who, for one hundred years or more, have tried to escape from the vast and splendid palaces imposed upon them by their inheritance. The Prince Consort early decided that "food always tastes better in small houses", and Queen Victoria liked to travel, incognito, through the Highlands, and stay in lonely inns. King Edward VII was more at home with his race-horses at Sandringham, than with his Van Dycks and Holbeins within the princely spaces of Windsor Castle. From the time that Queen Victoria bought Osborne in 1843, and built Balmoral in the early eighteen-fifties, our sovereigns have liked to escape from their palaces, to their houses, thus becoming an example in simplicity to their people.

We respect this simplicity, but we must also be grateful for the extravagant monarchs of the more distant past, who plunged their governments into debt so that they could build sumptuous palaces.

In writing of the King's "houses" we must pass quickly over Hampton Court and Kensington Palace, and write mostly of Buckingham Palace, Balmoral, Sandringham and Windsor Castle, between which the King divides his year. Buckingham Palace might be described as the London office of the monarchy, Balmoral the summer retreat, Sandringham the centre of English country pursuits, and Windsor the shrine of the King's history.

It is a pity that circumstances make Hampton Court unfit for the uses of contemporary

The South and East Fronts seen from near the Long Water

Above: The King's Staircase

Left: The State Bedroom
Right: The King's State Rooms

The King's Beasts

The Moat Bridge and the Western Gateway

The Fountain Court

The Clock Court Gateway

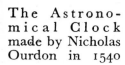

The Astronomical Clock made by Nicholas Ourdon in 1540

The Fountain Court, designed by Sir Christopher Wren

The Lion and the Unicorn on the Moat Bridge

Mars

The South Front, designed by Sir Christopher Wren

Hercules

The bust of Claudius: façade, Hampton Court Palace

monarchy, for no other scene near London would provide a weary king with such soothing escape from the cares of state. The echoes of Handel's Water Music are heard here, beside the

> . . . place which nature's choicest gifts adorn,
> Where Thames' kind streams in gentle currents turn,

and we may enjoy what remains of the palace as Wolsey built it; the "extensive palace" that "this butcher's cur" created in the height of his greatness. Even with the crowds and noises of a Saturday afternoon, it is impossible to wander in the ancient part of Hampton Court without gathering some notion of the state kept up by this "menial lord", with his "liveried army" of one thousand servants, attending 280 silk beds for his visitors; and the wagons arriving with the choicest food of the known world, to be prepared by the master cook, "attired daily in velvet" and wearing "a gold chain".

> In full-blown dignity see Wolsey stand
> Law in his voice, and fortune in his hand. . . .

A view of Hampton Court from the River Thames: from a seventeenth-century painting by Danckerts

KENSINGTON PALACE

We are tempted also to enjoy the modest beauty of Kensington Palace: the purple-red façade, with abundant chestnuts and liquid undulations of grass, still fitting the description, "a comfortable, homely suburban residence" given to it when Wren completed it at the end of the seventeenth century. Here are different ghosts, less in love with grandeur and fortune. They begin with King William III and Queen Mary, who occupied the house soon after their accession; and "Good Queen Anne, sitting in the sun". They include "a bright, pretty little girl of seven", born there in 1819. "The Duchess of Kent and her daughter . . . are breakfasting in the open air, a single page attending them. . . . The world of fashion is not yet astir, and the sun is scarcely high enough to have dried up the dews of Kensington's green alleys." It was in Kensington Palace that the same princess received the letter, in June 1837, "Keep your mind *cool* and *easy*; *be not alarmed* at the prospect of becoming, perhaps sooner than you expected, Queen". It was in Kensington Palace that she wrote in her diary, "I was awoke at six o'clock by Mamma . . . I got out of bed and went into my sitting-room (only in my dressing-gown) and *alone*". The age of dalliance was over and the long, secure, prosperous reign of Victoria had begun.

Christopher Wren was almost sixty years old when he began his work on Kensington Palace. Other architects made their pretentious additions in later years, but they left Wren's façade unspoiled, and, although part of the palace is now a museum, it keeps a quiet, domestic look, with little hint that anything has happened to it for almost one hundred years. There is an interesting collection of pictures in Kensington Palace, but it is my task only to awaken the human aspect of its story; the images that start to life as one stands on the steps and remembers that here Queen Victoria stood, in June 1867, when she went to see Queen Mary as a baby; when she paused and looked at the door knockers, and recalled that they were "old friends".

Queen Victoria's Bedroom

The Cupola Room

Queen Victoria's Nursery

SANDRINGHAM

One turns from the splendour of Hampton Court, and the quiet charm of Kensington Palace, to the youngest of the King's houses, Sandringham, in Norfolk. The building, in which King Edward VII and King George V found so much happiness, can claim less than a century of history. It was built, soon after Prince Albert Edward of Wales married Princess Alexandra, by a man with the uncompromising name of Goggs. The house is a sort of architectural wastrel and, as much as anything, it is inclined to be Elizabethan in design.

Over the front door is the inscription, "This house was built by Albert Edward and Alexandra his wife, in the year of Our Lord 1870". There Edwardian society gathered in all its superficial richness; to shoot pheasants, to admire *Persimmon*, with which the King won the Derby, and to enjoy the gardens he made, set amid well-bred lawns, stately trees, waterfalls and lakes. Here a king could enjoy the less arduous role of country squire, and if, in Edwardian days, older people thought the Court at Sandringham not very "nice", it was certainly a happy, self-satisfied society, the product of industrialism and prosperity.

Queen Victoria did not go to Sandringham very often, but there is the record of one visit which she enjoyed in 1889. On the last day the old Queen stayed up until 1 o'clock in the morning. Ellen Terry and Henry Irving had brought their company to Sandringham to act for her. "We sat in the front row," wrote the Queen, "the stage was beautifully arranged, and with great scenic effects, and the pieces splendidly mounted, with numbers of people taking part. I believe there were between sixty and seventy, as well as the orchestra. The piece, *The Bells*, is a melodrama . . . and is very thrilling." Queen Victoria thought that Irving "acted wonderfully", and that he was "very gentlemanlike". And Ellen Terry was both "pleasing and handsome".

"This house was built by Albert Edward and Alexandra his wife, in the year of Our Lord 1870"

BALMORAL

We step a little deeper into history when we come to the Deeside and see the towers of Balmoral, sheltered by larches, against the stern Scottish hills. The Prince Consort is continuously accused of having corrupted the æsthetic life of his time. He was a man of great knowledge, but less taste, and Mr. P. G. Wodehouse might have had him in mind when he wrote, "Whatever may be said in favour of the Victorians it is generally admitted that few of them were to be trusted within reach of a trowel and a pile of bricks". Balmoral Castle, with its Scottish baronial eccentricities, is a memorial to this mid-nineteenth-century fever for building. But there is more to Balmoral than this; it is a memorial also to the relationship between Queen Victoria and her husband. The Queen and Prince Albert first went to the Highlands in 1842, ten years before they began to build their own castle. This was the beginning of their obsession for everything Scottish; they found the Highlanders "such a chivalrous, fine, active people", and when they travelled south again they thought the English coast looked "terribly flat". They went to the Deeside every summer after this. In 1848 the Prince wrote, "We have withdrawn into . . . a complete mountain solitude, where one rarely sees a human face". In the evenings they dreamed and planned; the little Scottish castle which they rented stirred a wish for their own home, turreted and splendid, set in the placid majesty of the Highlands. In the summer of 1853 the new Balmoral Castle was "up one story", and in 1855 it was finished. Within, Prince Albert had wed his memories of German castles to his own taste, and the result was more enthusiastic than beautiful. The carpets were of tartan in honour of the Queen's descent from the Stuarts; even the linoleum in some of the rooms was tartan. The walls were lively with stags' heads that stared down at the unusual scene. One of the ladies-in-waiting wrote in a letter to her sister that the rooms were "all highly characteristic and appropriate but not equally *flatteux* to the eye". The first visit to the new castle ended in celebration. On September 8th, 1855, Sebastopol fell after a siege of three hundred and ninety-nine days. Prince Albert left his desk and walked out, to light a beacon, and to join the Scotsmen in "a veritable witch's dance, supported by whisky". It was at Balmoral that Prince William of Prussia picked a sprig of heather for the Queen's eldest daughter and asked her to be his wife; there that Florence Nightingale sat with the Queen and the Prince, telling them of the horrors of the Crimea. It was there that the Queen went, in 1862, in the terrible gloom of her widowhood. It was along the terrace of Balmoral that she walked with the Tsar and Tsarina of Russia, in October 1896, for an event which was a signal that her rich, safe century was ending: the Queen was photographed by what she called the "new cinematograph process" which made "moving pictures by winding off a reel of film".

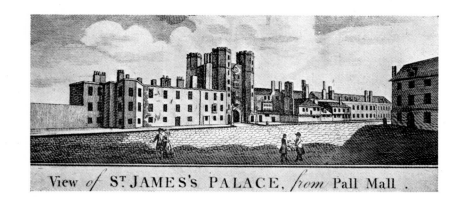

View of St JAMES's PALACE, from Pall Mall.

ST. JAMES'S PALACE

Henry VIII built the Manor House of St. James, which later became St. James's Palace, for the occupancy of Anne Boleyn

Above: The Armoury Room with its wall-panels decorated by William Morris

Right: The Elevations to the Colour Court

Left: The Friary Court

CLARENCE HOUSE

Clarence House is the home of Their Royal Highnesses, Princess Elizabeth and the Duke of Edinburgh. Right: The Garden Front. The two bays above the portico represent the south end of the house built by Nash in 1826–27 for the Duke of Clarence. The section to the right of the portico was added by the Duke of Edinburgh in 1875, when the whole was refaced and heightened. Below: The Drawing-room, the walls of which are painted ivory and pale grey and the ceilings, designed by Nash for the original house in 1825, are decorated in gold. The furniture was given to Their Royal Highnesses on their marriage. Other colours in the room are taken from two fine Aubusson carpets

The Grand Hall leading to the State Apartments, Buckingham Palace

BUCKINGHAM PALACE

We touch the fringe of a more exciting past when we come to the story of Buckingham Palace. But even here, it is of people rather than of architectural beauty that we think, as we gaze at the long façade of the King's London house.

The land on which Buckingham Palace is built was first notable as a "mulberry garden", in the reign of King James I, when the businesslike English were directing their attention "to the cultivation of silk worms as a profitable investment". The first house was built on the site in 1632; twenty-two years later it was a sort of public garden, and John Evelyn wrote of it as "the only place of refreshment about town for persons of the best quality". Samuel Pepys was not equally impressed; he thought it "a very silly place".

The first mansion was built for the Duke of Buckingham, early in the eighteenth century, from the designs of a Dutch architect. It was "a graceful palace, very commodious", and the Duke lived there until he died in 1720. Twenty-three years later, when his Duchess died, ". . . her effigy in wax . . . dressed up in her coronation robes, was placed under a canopy of state . . . with two ladies of her bedchamber at her head and feet, and drawn by six horses covered with black velvet". This effigy of the Duchess is still preserved among the relics in Westminster Abbey.

Buckingham House first became a Royal residence in 1761 when it was bought by King George III. The mansion then suffered so many structural changes that it reminded one visitor of "a country parsonage-house to which every incumbent has added something, one a washhouse, another a stable, another a hen-roost . . . till the whole is made a mere jumble of patchwork". The Palace may have lacked æsthetic appeal, but it achieved importance for other reasons. King George III formed a splendid library within the Palace and there many of the good and gifted men of the time gathered about their sovereign. The nicest record of such a meeting was written by Boswell, describing the conversation between George III and Dr. Johnson, in 1767.

Buckingham House in St. James's Park. From a contemporary engraving, *circa* 1714

The Throne Room

The White Drawing-room

Queen Victoria was already six years old when Nash began to build the Buckingham Palace of today. It was one of the least graceful of Nash's enterprises, and contemporary observers complained of "the feebleness of his ideas and the paltriness of his taste". After King George III died, the Palace was almost deserted: neither of his sons liked it, but it sparkled with life again in July 1837, when Queen Victoria moved there from her modest rooms in Kensington Palace.

One is tempted to enlarge on the stories of the spacious early-Victorian years: the Queen's coronation; the first exciting evenings when she danced until dawn came to the Palace gardens; the Sunday night dinners with kind, wise Lord Melbourne; her marriage, and the old travelling coach rattling out of the Palace courtyard to take her, with her bridegroom, to Windsor; the visit of Mendelssohn, when the Queen and Prince Albert joined him in

Doorway: The Picture Gallery

Fireplace: The Picture Gallery

The Blue Drawing-room

The Ceiling of the Blue Drawing-room

singing and playing; the collecting of fine pictures, and the building of the pavilion in the garden, in 1842, with frescoes by Landseer and his contemporaries of subjects "both moral and beautiful".

In 1851 an interesting architectural change was made to the Palace. It became necessary, as the Queen's family grew, to add a wing across the front. This required the removal of the marble arch, which dominated the entrance, so it was transplanted to the site it now occupies north of Hyde Park. The front of the Palace as we see it today is entirely modern; it was redesigned by Sir Aston Webb in 1912, to include the famous balcony on which the Royal family have so often appeared, to acknowledge the cheering of crowds below.

Her Majesty Queen Elizabeth in the White Drawing-room

Right: Looking from the balcony on which the Royal Family appear on great occasions

Below: Doorway leading from the Blue Drawing-room

The Thrones used by King George VI and Queen Elizabeth

Left: Looking from the middle window of the Balcony Room

Details from the coat-of-arms on the South Colonnade

Gateway
by night

Flood-lit
Façade

The Grand Entrance seen through the principal entrance in the main front

Details from the
coat-of-arms on
the South Colon-
nade

The Music Room

The domed ceiling of the Music Room

The State Dining-room

The Principal Corridor

A corner of the Music Room

Her Majesty Queen Elizabeth in the Blue Drawing-room

Cecil Beaton

WINDSOR

BARKSHIRE

WINDSOR CASTLE

In Windsor Castle, an imaginative monarch might become intimidated under the burden of his own history. For most of us, proud to find the letters of our name upon some mouldering graveyard stone, it is romantic that a constitutional sovereign of the twentieth century— a pilot in the R.A.F.—is able to pause in the shadow of these ancient walls and listen to so many voices; from the days of the Norman invader, the glorious age of Elizabeth, the tragedy of the Stuarts, the mixed blessing of the Georges, the complacent prosperity of Queen Victoria's reign, and from our own dangerous century, during which the castle has been defended with anti-aircraft guns emplaced in the park.

The architectural beginning of the Castle was simple and utilitarian. William the Conqueror cut trees from the forest and built a fortress on the lovely hill beside the Thames. Here he could police the valley, and perhaps enjoy sensations of power as he surveyed the landscape, laced by the river that carried the reflections of Oxford's spires, past Windsor, Hampton Court and London, to the open sea.

It is claimed that the immense and stately Castle of today, covering thirteen acres of high land, follows the same outline as the fortress of Norman times, which had towers at each corner and, within, a citadel of wood in which the garrison was housed.

It is not necessary to support this early history with legends, for there are records of William Rufus holding a council within the fortress as early as 1095. (Almost eight hundred and fifty years later, on the same ground, King George VI received his generals returned from victory in Europe.) After William Rufus had been killed in the New Forest, and buried "without prayer or knell", Henry I was at Windsor, planning great changes. The Conqueror

Left: The Quadrangle at Windsor Castle looking towards the Royal Apartments, with the equestrian statue of King Charles II by Stada

Above: The north elevation of Windsor Castle, *circa* 1570. From John Speed's Map of Berkshire. Left: The Keep floodlit

had made the hill-top into a defence; Henry I saw it as a home, so he transformed the walls from wood to stone, and built rooms, in which he lived with his second Queen, Adelaide of Louvain, whom he married at Windsor in 1121.

Henry II, who "did good justice and made peace", was also a great builder, and he gave the Castle its most imposing feature, the Round Tower. For those interested in stone construction the tower has especial interest. When you view it from the surrounding town of Windsor, it seems that the building is all one in age and craftsmanship. But when you stand close to the tower you detect a difference between the lower and upper structures—a difference in the shape and cutting of the stone. The lower half of the tower was built in 1172; the upper, six and a half centuries later, in the reign of George IV. The stone from which the Castle is built is so stout and impervious to weather, that time has had little effect on its texture or its colour.

There is one unhappy memorial to Henry II at Windsor—a reminder of the bitter and unnatural jealousy that so often estranges kings from their sons. Henry II "caused to be painted", on one of the walls, an old eagle, its eyes and body being scratched by four younger birds. The old eagle was himself, he said, and the four younger birds were his sons. He complained, "they cease not to pursue my death, and especially my youngest son John, whom now I love most, shall most especially await and imagine my death".

We move to the story of Richard Cœur de Lion; then to his brother, King John. The list of food and wine ordered for his Christmas celebrations in 1213 is interesting. He commanded "twenty tuns of good and new wine for the household, as well as Gascoigny and French wine, and four tuns of best wine for the King's own use". He also ordered "two hundred head of swine, one thousand capons, five hundred pounds of wax, fifty pounds of white bread, two pounds of saffron, one hundred pounds of good and fresh almonds, two dozen towels, one thousand yards of wove cloth to make table napkins, fifty yards of fine cloth of Rheims, and a sufficient quantity of spice for seasoning".

Nothing was left to chance in this early thirteenth-century housekeeping. Before King John arrived, the Sheriff of Buckinghamshire was ordered to purchase five hundred capons and twenty pigs for the Castle larder. Matthew Mantell had to find two hundred head of swine and one thousand capons, and John Fitz Hugh was commanded, "as he loved the King", to contribute "wood, coal, pitchers, cups and dishes, and a further five hundred capons". The stores were completed with a thousand salted eels, to be sent by the Sheriff of Kent.

It was to Windsor that John returned, in such rage that he "gnashed his teeth, rolled his eyes and gnawed sticks and straws", after being forced into accepting the Magna Carta at Runnymede. It is interesting, in these days of prolonged international councils, to recollect that these deliberations, which changed the shape of history, occupied nine days—before the arrogant monarch, who had declared, "By God's teeth I will not grant them liberties which will make me a slave", ultimately set his seal to the Great Charter.

The Castle had been damaged during the years of siege, before John's accession, and it fell to Henry III to restore its strength and beauty. We read of him, in 1243, planning to line his chamber with "boards, rayed and coloured". This was but a detail in his great building schemes, which went on, even in the twenty-fourth year of his reign, when he ordered a new apartment, sixty feet long and twenty-eight feet wide, to be built within the Castle. There were to be other new rooms, and a chapel, and it is an interesting light on the care

St. George's Chapel with the Round Tower in the background

and taste with which he made his plans that he wished enough space to be left between the new buildings "to make a grass plot".

The first king, recognisable to us as a man of breath and heart and mind—and not merely as a playing-card figure in two dimensions—is Edward III. *Edward of Windsor* he was often called, and rightly so, for, to this day, the Castle bears the fair imprint of his thought and idealism.

Edward III added rooms and towers of great splendour and made the Castle something of a palace, with a "chambre of mirrours" and a "dauncing chambre". The walls were painted in ochre and gilt, and, on the slopes below the Castle, jousts and tournaments were held. Among the records that survive is one of payment for "making one long and one short robe of six garniments of red velvet, for the lord the King, made, furred and purfled against the feast of the Round Table held at Windsor".

These garments were worn by Edward III for the festival out of which it might be said that the Order of the Garter was created; the oldest and most honourable order of chivalry in the world. Among those at the feast, in 1344, was Adam of Murimuth, who left a record of the proceedings. "At the costly banquet were the most alluring of drinks in plenty, enough and to spare. The lords and ladies failed not to dance, mingling kisses with embraces. . . . Many entertainers made the most charming melody and sundry other diversions. Some received changes in raiment, some gifts in abundance, some much gold and silver. On the fourth day the King began the Round Table; which done, trumpets and kettledrums

Above: The State Bedroom. Armour in the Guard Chamber. Left: The Waterloo Chamber. Right: Edward III's Coronation Chair, St. George's Hall

Above right: The Grand Staircase with the statue of King George IV, and beneath it the suit of armour made for Henry VIII in 1540. Above left: The Tricolour banner above the Duke of Wellington's bust in the Guard Chamber. Below right: The Van Dyck Room. Left: Queen Anne

sounded, and the guests hastened to a feast, complete with wealth of foods, variety of courses, and overflowing quantities of drink. The joy was unspeakable, the pleasure without murmuring, the hilarity without care."

The procession of Windsor's ghosts appears bewilderingly long as we turn over the pages of our history book, for almost every great Englishman, king or commoner, seems to have passed through the Castle gates. The Black Prince was married there, in 1361. Twenty-five years later, when "the whole country was much dissatisfied" with the rule of Richard II, men rode to Windsor, from London and the provinces, to remonstrate against the King's laws and taxes. It is curious to pause within the Castle walls today, with the crowds of democracy walking freely where they will, and imagine the proud, royal voice of the late fourteenth century, answering, "What we approve shall be granted, and what we think improper refused. For think not we are to be ruled by our people. That has never been. . . ."

Then came the melodramatic incidents of the reign of Henry IV; then the nine years of Henry V. During both these reigns James I of Scotland was kept a prisoner within the Castle, after being captured by an English ship off Flamborough Head in 1406. It was from his prison in the Maids of Honour tower that he first saw Jane Beaufort, in the "garden faire", with "hawthorn hedges knet" and the "sharp, green sweet juniper, growing so fair. . . ".

> And therewith cast I down mine eyes again,
> Where I saw walking under the tower,
> Full secretly, new comyn her to plain,
> The fairest and freshest young flower
> That e'er I saw. . . .

When he was released, and assumed his crown as King of Scotland, "the fairest and freshest young flower" became his queen.

The next figure that holds our attention is Henry VI, creator of Eton College, who was less than ten months old when the Great Seal of kingship was surrendered to him. He was ten years old when he returned to Windsor after a journey to Rouen, where he had been allowed to attend the trial of the Maid of Orleans. He was nineteen when he invited "all the faithful in Christ" to aid him in founding a college in the parish of Eton. The imaginative and creative mind that gave England both Eton College and King's, at Cambridge, trembled dangerously between talent and madness. Thirteen years after he ordered the building of Eton, King Henry VI lost his reason. There are records for the year 1454 of an "expert, notable and proved man in the craft of medicine", attending the King at Windsor to cure him of his "sickness and infirmityes". Henry VI ruled for thirty-nine years, and spent much of his time in the Castle, but no important changes were made to its structure during the reign. With the accession of Edward IV, Windsor prospered again, and in the thirteenth year of his reign he began to build the magnificent St. George's Chapel for the Knights of the Garter. Edward IV died at Westminster, but he demanded in his will that his body should be "buried in the Church of the College of Saint George within oure Castell of Wyndsore". The procession moves on: the brief reign of Edward V; then the summer of 1483, when Richard III stayed at Windsor for a few days after his coronation—two years before he "rushed into the thick of the fight,

Charles I

The Throne Room was designed for ceremonies of the Order of the Garter
The woodcarvings are by Grinling Gibbons

with his crown on his head, to meet a soldier's death" on Bosworth Field.

When Henry VII came to the throne, in 1485, he soon decided to make an interesting and splendid addition to the skyline of the Castle by erecting "heraldic supporters or symbols selected and taken from the Tudor dynasty to illustrate his claim through both the rival houses of York and Lancaster to be in direct lineal descent from Edward III, Founder of the Order of the Garter."

These heraldic beasts, each about four feet high, were carved in stone and added to the pinnacles of St. George's Chapel. There is an amusing record of this work, which shows that the contractors had a sternly business-like conception of the value of sculpture. The beasts were carved at "the rate of 6s. 8d. the foote". The cost for "carv^g 6 Beasts Royall" was £13 17s. 6d.

For almost two hundred years these stone figures crowned St. George's Chapel, while much of England's history was being woven in the great Castle below. The stone animals began to crumble and, during the reign of Charles II, Christopher Wren was called in to make a report on them. He wrote:—"The beasts on the West body of the Church which are all decayed, and by falling break the lead of the roof, might be taken off; and in lieu of them stone pineapples be added to coape the pinnacles, for the advantage it would give the fabric." Only part of Wren's advice was followed. The carved beasts were removed, but the stone pineapples were

William III

the great collections of paintings and drawings that had been scattered during the Commonwealth; he engaged Peter Lely to paint portraits, Verrio to decorate the ceilings and walls, and Grinling Gibbons to carve. He planted rows of trees, and built a summer house at Datchet, so that he could fish for salmon in the Thames. He stocked the forest with deer, and he built a tennis court. We read of him in August 1679 playing "a long, hot game of tennis" and, after being "rubbed down", walking "in the cool of the evening beside the river". He was "taken sick" after this indiscretion, "with a shivering ague and high fever". We read of Pepys and John Evelyn going to Windsor in the summer of 1674, to see a representation of the taking of Maestricht in a meadow below the Castle. Evelyn wrote in his diary, "The siege being over, I went with Mr. Pepys back to London, where we arrived about three in the morning".

Near the Castle, in King Charles's time, was a house which he built for Nell Gwynn, and it is incongruous to note that after the favourite had left, the next occupant was Queen Anne—before she was queen. After she was crowned she lived many years at Windsor, with her husband, so sadly described by Charles II, "I've tried him drunk and I've tried him sober, but there's nothing in him". But there was one splendid moment in Windsor's story associated with Queen Anne. Overlooking the north terrace is a window at which she liked to sit; it was there that the news of the Battle of Blenheim was brought to her in 1704.

Anne died in 1714, and the great Castle was allowed to decay. The early Georges did not seem to care for living there and it was not until the reign of George III that Windsor resumed its dignity as the King's house. George III did great things for the Castle; he added to the collection of pictures, he summoned musicians there, he restored St. George's Chapel and, after he had been living there some eighteen years, he planned the great restoration of the Castle, which was finished by George IV. It was on October 1, 1823, that King George IV "made a triumphal entry into the town" when "oxen and sheep were roasted whole, the poorer classes dined in public in the High Street, the houses were illuminated, fireworks displayed, and a grand ball and entertainment given at the Town Hall".

The moral sins of kings are interred with their bones, but the palaces they build live after them, and we must be grateful to King George IV for many extravagances; the Pavilion at Brighton, the redecoration of Buckingham Palace, the building of Carlton House, and much of the restoration of Windsor. He removed some of the charm from the conglomeration of unrelated structures that must have seemed like history told in stone. But he made

Windsor Castle. View from the north, showing Queen Elizabeth's new Terrace. From Marcus Gerard's

Proceeding of the Sovereign and Knights Companions of the Order of the Garter at St. George's Feast in 1578

Windsor Castle: Approach Gate, Castle Hill

the Castle into a habitable and imposing palace by massing the confused buildings into a whole, with towers and battlements to give it a brave and gallant look. Within, he built passages to join the rooms, and added every luxury that was discovered in his time.

King George IV died in Windsor Castle. "My boy, this is death", he murmured to his doctor. And he was buried at Windsor, which remains much as he made it; much as we see it now. So the story moves into the times of our great-grandfathers. The centuries of cruelty, of ruthless splendour, and of monarchy that existed as something apart from ordinary humanity, were over. We recognize something of our own life as we read of Windsor, in February 1840. The travelling coach that had left Buckingham Palace at four o'clock in the afternoon, came to Windsor town. The two occupants looked out and noticed that the houses "glowed with crowns, stars, and all the brilliant devices which gas and oil could supply".

The coach passed under the arch and stopped in the upper quadrangle of the Castle that had been the fortress, then the home, of kings, for almost eight hundred years. A new history, which is our history, began with that winter evening at Windsor, one hundred and eleven years ago, when Queen Victoria wrote in her journal, "I and Albert, alone".

ROYAL PAVILION

by REX DE C. NAN KIVELL

IN talk and literature, castles and palaces have as their associates kings and princes, and in the building of these places there has been, in general, a recognisable aspect of period and condition. Often it may be a king is wise in accepting the suggestions of his advisors, and so become historically the originator. When, therefore, a king creates an architectural fantasy, all must wonder and ask what manner of man is this.

With the creation of the Royal Pavilion at Brighton, we have the satisfaction of knowing that the brain of George, Prince of Wales, later the Prince Regent, later King George IV, was picturing and selecting the host of details necessary in every addition made, and always naturally visualising himself personally in association with the finished effect.

The Pavilion, as created, was so essentially a personal foible that it could never be repeated successfully as a style, and so we cannot help enjoy it simply for what it is—a breath of that gaiety and charm for which we all search but so rarely find. All intelligent people want to build their own Pavilions; but it took a Prince, with his power, to build this existing one, which is surely a comet in comparison to our star-like dreams.

The secret of its success is greatly helped by the knowledge that the craftsmen who did the many necessary jobs believed in the objects they were creating; there were no short cuts taken anywhere to try to achieve the same effect, and all the work was done beautifully. We can easily imagine the numberless times of trial and error when matching the tones of the paintwork, whether it be silver or gold lines, the colour and pattern of the draperies, the carpets, Oh, every smallest item.

The Prince Regent, yes, was happy to have had men like Holland, Porden, Repton, Nash and Lambalet as assistants to his purpose in evolving a seaside villa into the most astonishing and original Oriental Pavilion that exists in Europe. There was only one source from which the builders could have been so impetuously swept along in the excitement of fulfilment, and that was the Prince Regent himself. So profound was the Prince Regent's interest in his creation that he designed his own Oriental robes to be worn inside the building, and went so far as to insist that the Royal family and friends, when on a visit to him at Brighton, appear also in Oriental costumes at his dinner-table.

The interior selected for illustration here is "The Banqueting Room," and on seeing even this reproduction one is at once carried into the romance of a fairy story but with real people in a glittering, unreal setting. The genius of creating a metal and glass and painted arbour inside four walls is something so unexpected and beautiful that one immediately is in complete oblivion to one's own world. The fascination of exploring this new illusion is overwhelming and seemingly never ending. After twenty years' acquaintance with the Royal Pavilion one is still under its spell.

A few dates will help the reader to put the construction of the Pavilion into perspective. George, Prince of Wales, first visited Brighton on Sunday, 7th September, 1783, when he

The Banqueting Room, the Royal Pavilion, Brighton, designed by John Nash, Esq., Architect, during one of the splendid entertainments given by the Prince Regent. "Creating, in mid-air, a diamond blaze," the glittering room is dominated by a lustre of immense size, thirty feet high, festooned with jewellery, suspended from the claws of a dragon

was twenty-one. He took up residence in a house which was later pulled down to make way for the extension of the Music Room of the present Pavilion. In 1785 he married Mrs. FitzHerbert, and in 1786 went to Brighton with her.

The first "Marine Pavilion" built by Henry Holland, was of a simple classical design and was finished in 1787. This building still forms the nucleus of the present Pavilion.

In 1795, the Prince's debts being £640,000, his father, King George III, refused to settle them unless he agreed to repudiate his marriage with Mrs. FitzHerbert and contract an alliance which could be officially recognised. Against his own inclinations the Prince of Wales did this and married his cousin, Princess Caroline of Brunswick, on the 8th of April, 1795. In June they both went to Brighton.

It was between the years 1801–04 that the startling alterations of spires and canopies and domes were carried out by P. F. Robinson, one of Holland's assistants. The Chinese influence was now to become the feature of the interior, and in fact persisted through all the changes of architects and decorators. In 1808 the style of the exterior additions and alterations was evolving from the Chinese to the Indian, and in 1815 John Nash began his great changes in design which exist in the building today. Alterations, improvements and embellishments to the interior were still being pushed on with increasing activity. In 1818 the Banqueting Room was nearly finished and also the organ for the Music Room, but even with these approaching completions more alterations were projected! The new alterations were to be most extensive and were expected to extend over two years! Apparently ever unfinished and unfinishable. Surely the Prince Regent's ideas of happiness must have been in anticipation, not in enjoyment!

The Prince Regent succeeded his father in January 1820, and it was in January 1821 that the Pavilion was completed sufficiently for the new King to move in. At this date the grandeur of the Brighton Pavilion was the talk of all the Continental court circles, and many of the visiting monarchs to England paid visits to Brighton to view the work in progress.

One is left with astonishing surmises as to the ultimate fate of the design and decoration of the Royal Pavilion if a greater hand had not taken charge and stopped for ever on June 25th, 1830, the devious and delicious fantasies that were constantly being created and changed by King George IV.

William IV and Queen Caroline paid many visits to the Pavilion and some alterations still took place, but when Queen Victoria came to the throne her visits were very few. Sad news was heard in 1844, that the Royal Pavilion was not to be used again by Her Majesty, and between 1846–47 the work of dismantling the building was begun and vigorously carried on. Why? One wonders what interest or pleasure could be obtained, and by whom, and for what purpose. Walls were stripped, mantelpieces were torn away from the walls, the furnishings dispersed and even the plants in the Royal garden were sold by auction in April 1848. In 1849 the Commissioners of Woods and Forests, who at that date had control of such Royal buildings as the Pavilion, brought before the House of Commons a Bill to authorise them "to sell—or to pull down—the Pavilion". Be it ever to the glory of those people of Brighton who at their Town Meeting, when on hearing of this Bill, voted in favour of buying the Royal Pavilion for the town of Brighton.

It was in 1863, in response to the entreaties of Mr. P. E. de Val, the Custodian of that date, that Queen Victoria returned a great deal of the decorations and fittings which had not been incorporated in the reconstructions of Buckingham Palace, and in later years Queen Mary has had returned several ornaments which have been identified as Pavilion objects. Many of the most exciting pieces of furniture, and mantelpieces, are still in Buckingham Palace; one wonders if they feel as happy there in conjunction with their present surroundings as they did in their original positions.

From the beginnings of the buildings to the end of the reign of its creator the expenditure on the Royal Pavilion and estate, including the purchase of land and property, additions, repairs and most of the decorations and furnishing, amounted to a total cost of £502,797 6s. 10d. One reads there was public lament on this so-called public extravagance, but was a unique enterprise such as this an extravagance in comparison to, say, four or more millions of pounds spent on a modern battleship which, in perhaps less than twenty years, is obsolete and sure destined to "scrap" and about which there is never a murmur of public disapproval?

If only there could now be other creators of fantasies such as the "Royal Pavilion", the world surely would be happier for us, and if there cannot be, let us thank the Prince Regent for having created the greatest of them all.

THE
KING'S PICTURES

BY GRACIOUS PERMISSION OF HIS MAJESTY THE KING

Van Dyck   Charles I

DENYS SUTTON

The Trinity Altarpiece by Hugo van der Goes. James III of Scotland and his Son

THE
KING'S
PICTURES

DENYS SUTTON

The Trinity Altarpiece. Margaret of Denmark, Queen of Scotland. Holyrood Palace

THE STUDY of painting in England would be immeasurably poorer without the existence of the collection of pictures and drawings formed over many generations by members of the Royal family. Today, when so much has been dispersed, it remains the most important collection of old masters in private hands and a remarkable testimony to the love of art which has persisted in this country. The treasures assembled from the various Royal residences, from Windsor Castle, from Hampton Court and from Buckingham Palace, formed, indeed, the theme of one of the most exciting exhibitions ever to have been held at the Royal Academy (in 1946–47).

It is a collection which may be enjoyed for its own sake, as a survey of European art which contains masterpieces that grace the pages of many volumes, and lesser works which provoke the attention of the historian and connoisseur. It also provides a fascinating panorama of the development of taste and reflects some of those changes in artistic appreciation which have occurred in England. It is not a collection that has been formed by one man alone, as hardly needs emphasis; it is a family collection which has been expanded or not according to the personality of the incumbent of the throne at a particular moment. Many factors have assisted in its formation and included in it are paintings which have been brought together through dynastic reasons, through chance and by choice. Broadly speaking, it consists of two main sections: those works which have been directly commissioned from contemporary artists or bought in their lifetime, and which consequently suggest the degree of patronage at a given epoch, and those paintings which have been collected by artists of established reputations.

In a sense, then, the Royal collection is a reflection of the history of English taste and to some degree even of English art with all its limitations and particularities. As much as anything else, however, it demonstrates, if that were necessary, the extent to which works of art have been loved in this country. The Royal collection is a lasting expression of that passion for possession which may be seen in the great collections, formed by nobleman and commoner alike, in the past. In a continuous manner it reveals the desire to decorate the interior which has been so characteristic of English life and which has contributed to the creation of those palaces and country houses, such as Knole, Longleat, Chatsworth and Blenheim, which have rightly been described as our most significant contribution to the visual arts. It is this combination of elements within one collection which makes its examination so fascinating and which makes the lover of art grateful to monarchs whose political capabilities are sometimes disputed. Whatever the verdict of posterity as to the sagacity of Charles I or George IV may be, their taste will not be disputed. The extravagance of Charles I, the groans of his bankers when forced to meet still more bills incurred by the purchase of works of art, or the debts and domestic dramas of George IV, may never be denied; they may secure the criticism of the moralist. Yet without their particular natures they might never have felt the urge to possess, and the results of their acquisitiveness are amongst the most exciting and rewarding jewels of a splendid heritage.

The Royal collection as it now stands is, however, only a part of what it might have been. It must be seen against its background and its past. Such catastrophes as the sale of Charles I's collection by the Commonwealth, or the great fire that occurred in William III's reign, have robbed the collection of many important works. Nor when the theme of Royal patronage and collecting is considered must one forget the decoration of palaces, amongst others the magnificent ceiling decorations by Rubens for the Banqueting House, Whitehall, which is one of the masterpieces of the Northern Baroque. It is a knowledge of these monuments that would assist us to receive a picture of the variations of Royal taste and the collection must be considered as part of that vast enterprise in artistic patronage which has inevitably been the concern of the monarch.

Much that would be germane to an assessment of Royal taste lies in other directions, in architecture, in gardening, in sculpture, and thus lies outside the scope of this particular examination. It is for such reasons that the origins of the Royal collection of pictures are to be found only as late as Henry VIII. Naturally enough, the English kings were concerned with painting before that period, but their achievements lie elsewhere and, though much has been destroyed, a measure of their taste may be seen in Westminster Abbey and in such chapels as Eton or St. George's, Westminster. Our conception of the history and state of the arts in England would be broadened if it were now possible to see the great mural decorations carried out for Richard II in the Palace of Westminster and in which foreign artists from France, Italy and elsewhere collaborated. Yet something of the gracious quality of late medieval art, as it appealed to Richard II, may be seen in the Wilton Dyptich (National Gallery), which is the most exquisite English painting of the period, or in his portrait in Westminster Abbey. Those works which do survive from this period, notably the great altarpiece by Hugo van der Goes (Page 92) (National Gallery of Scotland), with its portraits of James III of Scotland and his wife, indicates that one of the major achievements of Royal patronage, whether north or south of the border, has been to introduce a knowledge of Continental styles into the country. The possession of wealth, the opportunity to travel themselves or to employ agents, and dynastic alliances have meant that Royal collectors—Charles, George IV or Richard II—have looked abroad and not

King Henry VIII
(1491-1547),
after Hans Hol-
bein. Windsor
Castle

The Battle of
Pavia. German
School. Hampton
Court Palace

remained content with an indigenous production. The result has been to effect a transmission of artistic styles and to broaden the artistic basis of our island culture.

The need for the introduction of some outside influence was particularly necessary in the England of the Tudors after the ravages caused by the Wars of the Roses. The effect upon the Court of such a perfect Italian High Renaissance picture as Raphael's *St. George* (National Gallery, Washington), must have been remarkable. It was sent by the Duke of Urbino to Henry VII as a gift to thank him for the Order of the Garter. It was this exchange of presents amongst the rulers that assisted in the fertilisation of English painting itself, and presumably some of the early portraits, listed in the Inventories of the collection of Henry VIII, were already owned by his father.

The Battle of the Spurs, 1513   Hampton Court Palac

Adam and
Eve, by
Mabuse,
1503–1536.
Collection
Henry VIII.
Hampton
Court
Palace

One of the most fascinating aspects of the Royal collection of pictures is the possibility of determining when particular paintings were purchased. This may be established by a considerable body of documents—early inventories, printed catalogues and eye-witness accounts. On the basis of such documents it is possible to indicate, with a reasonable degree of certainty, the taste of a King and to provide a knowledge of those pictures available in England during his lifetime. The earliest of these inventories is of the collection of Henry VIII, compiled in 1542. Henry's interest in works of art was natural. The moment was ripe for an extension of artistic activity in England, and the artistic achievements on the Continent were such as to excite so expansive a personality as the King, with his love of life in all its forms. His sense of decoration and his capacity for entertainment appeared in his feats at the celebrations of the Field of the Cloth of Gold and, like Francis I, he felt that he, too, should have his painters and his palaces, a view shared by Cardinal Wolsey, a prince of the Church whose patronage was equally extensive. Henry had the singular good fortune to employ Holbein, whose work in England includes the famous portrait drawings at Windsor and various other portraits. Unfortunately, some of his finest paintings have been destroyed, including the portrait-group at Whitehall, which was a fitting expression of the dominating personality of the King. He liked his portraits large and imposing and, according to Carel van Mander, visitors on entering the Royal Chamber were startled by a life-like portrait greeting them which they took to be the King himself. Fundamentally, Henry's approach to painting was utilitarian, and Italian artists, such as Vincent Volpe, were employed to draw the pennants of the Royal ships, notably the *Royal Harry*, in 1514. It was significant of the period, too, that the collection contained a number of pictures illustrating religious controversy, and such paintings as *The Pope stoned by four Evangelists*, indicates the use of painting for propaganda. Yet the Royal collection at this date also contained such remarkable works as Mabuse's *Adam and Eve* (Page 95), and Holbein's *Noli me tangere*.

As a full-blooded Renaissance monarch, Henry's tastes were luxuriant, thugho tempered by the needs of his particular situation. His immediate successors to the throne, however, lacked his gusto and their additions to the collection were few. Yet the lines for the future development of patronage and collecting were now established. Besides Holbein, some Italian artists had worked in England, such as Girolamo de Treviso and Toto della Nunziata whose painting provided Englishmen "with what might be called a résumé of contemporary Italian tendencies". The influence of such work, brought over through the Royal agency, was important, and one must not forget that throughout the Tudor period, when art was focused on, and largely controlled by, the Court, no strong native tradition of painting existed. The results of the patronage of Henry VIII, Edward VI and Mary, and the works of the few native painters working in England, formed the nucleus of the collections of the late sixteenth and early seventeenth centuries. In any case, by Elizabeth's accession, the English Court was considered as a possible market for works of art, and a French dealer, Nicholas Houel, attempted to sell a collection containing some works by Dürer to Queen Elizabeth. At this time Hilliard and Isaac Oliver were miniaturists of great talent, but no artistic activity existed compatible to the literary renaissance of the epoch, and no corresponding treasures entered the Royal collection. No first-rate painter arrived in England, though the customary portraits were acquired by the Tudors. The same was true of the reign of James I, and the Court painters were Van Somer and Daniel Mytens. All the

Above: Queen Elizabeth confounding Juno,
Minerva and Venus, by Hans Eworth (*c.*
1520–after 1578). An ingenious piece of Court
flattery: the picture is a *Judgement of Paris*
brought up to date, with the Orb for the apple,
and Queen Elizabeth for Paris, who surprises
the goddesses by awarding the prize to herself.
A view of Windsor Castle is seen behind. Now
in Hampton Court Palace, this picture was in
the Royal Collection until the Commonwealth
sale, and recovered at the Restoration

Right: Henry, Prince of Wales (1594–1612)
and Lord Essex, attributed to Marc Gheeraerts
(*c.* 1562–1636). The Prince is about to deliver
the *coup de grâce* to a stag whose antlers are held
by Lord Essex. This was probably a presenta-
tion picture to the Prince. Hampton Court
Palace

same, conditions were gradually prepared for the great artistic triumphs of Charles I's reign.

Even now, when some of the finest works acquired by Charles I are no longer amongst the Royal pictures, it is possible to realise the immense splendour of the artistic patronage of this particular reign, and in the imagination one can create a capital and a gallery of fantastic treasures. England itself was at the beginning of a period of expansion, and all those tendencies of admiration for Italian culture and the cult of Neo-Platonism which had emerged with Henry VIII or under Elizabeth came to fruition. It is equally significant that the collections of the King and his great nobles were formed at a time when England had begun to play an important part in the commercial life of Europe, and the internationalism of the era, apparent in literature, also manifests itself in collecting. The appearance in England of the great collections must be viewed against the economic background, when the purchase of works of art in different countries was facilitated by the existence of agents and bankers. Now, as in no other era of our history, Charles and some of his leading subjects—Lord Arundel and the Duke of Buckingham—and flanked by their assistants— Inigo Jones, Lanière, Nys—formed the pivot on which centred the artistic activity of almost all England and a part of the Continent. Charles' interest in works of art had been foreshadowed by his elder brother Henry, Prince of Wales, who at the age of fifteen had acquired the great library from Nonesuch, and who "brought over several valuable works of great masters from all countries". He died too young to show his true character as a collector, but some paintings have been identified as belonging to him, amongst them the portrait of him and the young Lord Essex (Page 97). It was at this period, too, that Inigo Jones built a special room at Whitehall for the picture collection.

Charles grew up then in a generation which was marked by a strong interest in the fine arts, which was spread by men older than him, such as Lord Arundel and Inigo Jones. The growth of his taste was doubtless assisted by his friendship with the Duke of Buckingham, an omnivorous collector, with whom he visited Madrid in his attempt to secure the hand

King Charles I (1600–1649) in Three Positions, by Sir Anthony van Dyck (1599–1641). Painted for the sculptor Bernini in Rome, so that he could make a bust without seeing the King. From Windsor Castle

Caesar's Chariot, a detail from *The Triumph of Caesar* by Mantegna.
Hampton Court Palace

of Philip IV's sister. His Royal host presented him with some magnificent pictures, above all by Titian, and he certainly acquired at this time Titian's *Girl with a Fur Cap* (Vienna Gallery), an artist of whom he was always to nourish a strong affection. He was also in touch with various private collections, and significant of the future was the presence in Buckingham's suite of Balthasar Gerbier, the agent, painter and go-between who helped to buy works of art for the Duke.

On his accession in 1625, Charles devoted greater energy to the formation of his collection, and he was well served by a group of agents, including Daniel Nys, who may well be the author of a small still-life at Hampton Court, and Nicholas Lanière, as well as by his ambassadors and members of the diplomatic corps, who were at all times instructed to keep their eyes alert for works of art. The efforts of his agents had their rewards, and against the competition of the Grand Duke of Tuscany, the Queen Mother of France and Cardinal Richelieu, Nys and Lanière were able to purchase, for a huge price, the collection of Vincenzo Gonzaga, Duke of Mantua. This included Mantegna's *Triumph of Caesar* (above), Tintoretto's *Nine Muses* (Page 101), and an impressive selection of the Italian masters of the Renaissance. With pardonable pride, Nys wrote home to Endymion Porter that "the Princes of Christendom, both great and small, were struck with astonishment

St. George and the Dragon, by Sir Peter Paul Rubens, 1577–1640.   Collection Charles I: Buckingham Palace

A detail from St. George and the Dragon, showing how Rubens painted the Saint and the Princess in the likeness of Charles I and Henrietta Maria. The scene is set on the banks of the Thames

The Nine Muses, by Jacopo Tintoretto, 1518–1594. Collection Charles I: Hampton Court Palace

Cupid and Psyche, by Sir Anthony van Dyck (1599–1641). Collection Charles I: Hampton Court Palace. Cupid finds Psyche, who has been struck down after opening the casket of beauty

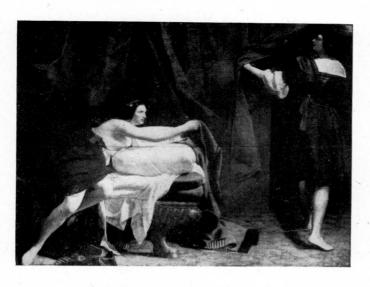

Left: Joseph and Potiphar's Wife, by Orazio Gentileschi (1562–1647). Collection Charles I: Hampton Court Palace

Right: Self-portrait by Artemisia Gentileschi (1597–after 1651). Collection Charles I: Hampton Court Palace

The Marriage of St. Catherine, Veronese (1528–1588). Collection: Part of a Dutch gift to Charles II: Hampton Court Palace

Above: A YOUNG MAN IN RED, by a Follower of Hans Holbein, collection of Charles II, Hampton Court Palace. Top right: A KNIGHT OF MALTA, by Tintoretto (1518–1594), Hampton Court Palace, collection of Charles I. Right centre: PORTRAIT OF A MAN, known as Jacopo Sannazaro, by Titian (c. 1485/8–1576), collection of Charles II, Hampton Court Palace. Bottom right: DERICH BORN, by Hans Holbein the Younger (1497–1543), collection of Charles II, Windsor Castle

JOHANN ZOFFANY, R.A., 1733–1810
Windsor Castle

QUEEN CHARLOTTE
Painted for George III

SIR ANTHONY VAN DYCK, 1599–1641
Windsor Castle

THE VILLIERS BOYS
Probably painted for Charles I

EUROPA
Collection George IV

CLAUDE LORRAIN
Buckingham Palace

Self-portrait
Sir Peter Paul Rubens,
Collection Charles I
Windsor Castle

Shepherd with Pipe
Giorgione, 1478–1510
Collection Charles I
Hampton Court Palace

Portrait of a Boy
Parmigianino, 1504–1540
Collection Charles II
Windsor Castle

Portrait of Isabella d'Este by
Giulio Romano, 1492–1546.
A Dutch gift to Charles II.
Hampton Court Palace. The
detail (*above*) shows the
inner room in right back-
ground; a maid admits three
visitors to the Marchesa's
apartments through a cur-
tained portal

SIR PETER LELY, 1618-1680
Hampton Court Palace

ELINOR, LADY BYRON
Collection Charles II

SIR ANTHONY VAN DYCK
Windsor Castle

THOMAS KILLIGREW AND THOMAS CAREW
Collection James II

that we could induce the Duke of Vincenzo to dispose of them". The collection cost the then immense sum of eighteen thousand, and doubtless expenditure of this nature contributed to the embarrassment of the King's finances. Philip Burlamachi, the banker who dealt with Charles, wrote with some bitterness, "If it were for two or three thousand it could be borne". Yet the Royal appetite for pictures was not to be assuaged; two years after the acquisition of the Mantua collection, Charles purchased *The Acts of the Apostles*, the seven magnificent cartoons for tapestry by Raphael that are now in the Victoria and Albert Museum. Besides the acquisition of collections *en bloc* or such imposing sets as the Raphael cartoons, Charles was constantly adding smaller collections, such as that of Froschl, or single pictures, and as a true collector was always happy to embark on an exchange, as when he gave the Raphael *St. George* to Lord Pembroke for the volume of Holbein drawings. On another occasion he received Leonardo da Vinci's *St. John the Baptist* from Louis XIII in exchange for a Holbein and a Titian.

Whatever Charles' fault as man and monarch, his artistic sensibility was profound, and his taste and patronage benevolent and influential, both in art and letters, and the establishment of the Mortlake tapestry works was due to his inspiration. He was, as an early writer on English art correctly said, "not only the greatest favourer but the truest knower of all

The Gerbier Family, by Sir Peter Paul Rubens (1517–1640), purchased by Frederick, Prince of Wales, now in Windsor Castle. This portrait group shows Sir Balthasar Gerbier, his wife and nine children, and was originally bought in Flanders as a work of Van Dyck. The group of the mother, the baby and the three children next to her, formed the centre of the original composition, and is different in treatment from Gerbier with his dog on the left and from the girls climbing the steps. The girl holding up her apron is only partly finished, and was probably so when Rubens died in 1640

The detail shows one of the children added by another painter, and the carved stone vase with Gerbier's coat-of-arms in relief

Augusta, Princess of Wales, and her Six Elder
Children, by Barthelemy du Pan (1712–1763).
Painted for Frederick, Prince of Wales, this picture
is in Windsor Castle. The setting is the garden of
the Prince of Wales's house at Park Place, Henley

Princess Louisa Ann, by Jean-Etienne Liotard
(1702–1789), is one of nine companion portraits of
the children of Frederick, Prince of Wales, and
were painted for Augusta, Princess of Wales.
Among her accounts at Windsor, where the portraits
are today, is a bill from Liotard, dated 15. viii.
1755, for 108 guineas, which is for some of these

those Arts and by his Countenance the whole Court gave themselves to those refined pleasures: there being hardly a man of great quality that had not a collection of Pictures or Antiques. Artists flowed in upon us from all parts".

It was one of Charles' virtues that he was not content to accumulate the masters of the past, but that he played his part as a patron of modern art. And he was lucky in the artists he called upon to serve him. Van Dyck's many portraits of the King—the famous three heads painted for Bernini (Page 98), or the equestrian portrait (Page 91)—have expressed for all times an image of a courtly, romantic King, a chivalrous knight and the flower of a particular style of living that was to disappear before the impact of a harder era. During the nine years he spent here and enjoyed the favour of the King or the Court, Van Dyck, who could turn from the portrait to the platonic cult of Henrietta Maria, which may be rendered in his *Cupid and Psyche* (Page 101), succeeded, above all else, in formulating a style of portrait painting, presenting the image of the courtly lady and gentleman, realistic but romantic, which was to set the tone for over a hundred years and which, in its own way, indicated, even after he had died, the imposition of the Caroline way of life upon posterity.

It is not difficult to believe that Charles enjoyed the company of Van Dyck and Rubens. His intercourse with such men, as indeed with Inigo Jones, must have assisted in broadening his taste. One of the most remarkable aspects of the King is just this wide range of his artistic interests. His love for the Venetians, whose sumptuous qualities matched the verses of Spenser and the luxurious nature of the Court, was understandable enough, and who could fail to succumb to their colours, pristine as they then were. But it was typical of his nature that he should have owned a Rembrandt and have been a great admirer of German and Flemish painting. Conversation, one may well imagine, turned upon such topics when Charles and Rubens had the opportunity of meeting when the latter was in London, in 1636, as an emissary of the Spanish Court, which is yet another indication of the close relationship between art and diplomacy at this epoch. Rubens himself, vital, learned and courtly, was just the man to appeal to English taste, and with him they could feel the link with the great tradition of High Renaissance Italian decoration. The echoes of the Veronese that appear in the paintings he executed for the Whitehall ceiling certainly confirmed their judgment. Still in existence, these magnificent and enormous panels were painted for Inigo Jones' Banqueting House in Whitehall, and designed to illustrate the reign of James I. A masterpiece of Northern Baroque, it not only symbolised Charles' views of kingship, but indicated the immense ability with which Rubens could translate a theme into painting. It was equally in keeping with the allegorical nature of the age that Rubens should have represented Charles and Henrietta Maria in his painting of *St. George* (Page 100), which the artist gave to the King on leaving the country.

Van Dyck and Rubens were the two leading artists patronised by Charles, and some of their most impressive works were bought or commissioned by the King or have entered the Royal possession at a subsequent date. Charles was equally interested in the then rather daring and modern work of the Tuscan Orazio Gentileschi, a follower of Caravaggio, and thus of the international style of chiaroscuro which had such an effect in early seventeenth-century Europe. Charles sent for him in about 1629, and Gentileschi, as well as Rubens, participated in the King's grand design to decorate his palaces. He was commissioned to paint the Queen's House at Greenwich and some of his paintings are still there, while others are at Marlborough House. There is about his painting, such as *Potiphar's*

Wife (Page 102), a theatrical and almost morbid quality which recalls the heated, dramatic world of Webster. Whatever we may now think of Gentileschi's painting, and it is now perhaps more in favour than it was some years ago, it must be taken into consideration in any examination of Charles' taste.

He was, in any case, yet another pillar of that careful fabric of artistic endeavour which Charles carefully constructed and which the Civil War effectively shattered. One of the results of the King's defeat was the sequestration in 1649 of the Royal possessions. With wanton disregard for the future, the Commonwealth arranged a sale of the pictures and other effects, the details of which are still obscure. Such an opportunity was not missed by collectors on the Continent, and many of the principal amateurs of the period—the King of Spain, Archduke Leopold William, Cardinal Mazarin, the banker Jabach and the brothers Van Reynst—were represented, and waggon loads of pictures set off from our shores. Many of the finest works, including such masterpieces as Titian's *Venus with an Organ Player* (Prado), subsequently entered the collections of the Prado, the Louvre and the Vienna Gallery. Fortunately, though many magnificent pictures were lost forever, inventories were taken of the collection which enable us to enjoy, even in retrospect, the splendours of the Royal collection, and they form one of the sure means of identifying those works which actually were in the Royal collection. There is still much research to be accomplished in relation to the sale, and much may be gleaned regarding the taste and values of the times. Some of the pictures, however, were reserved for Cromwell, including Mantegna's *Triumph* and the Raphael cartoons, which were given the extremely low valuation of three hundred pounds. The Correggio, however, was valued at one thousand pounds and Raphael's *La Perla* at two thousand. The list of Cromwell's choice includes, as Anthony Blunt has remarked, "several Madonnas and an Assumption, surprising subjects for the head of a Puritan State".

Cromwell's triumph witnessed not only the defeat of the Royal cause, but it dealt a

CANALETTO, 1697–1768

Windsor Castle

A VIEW OF THE RIVER THAMES

JAN STEEN, 1626–1679   THE MORNING TOILET
Buckingham Palace   Collection the Prince Regent

bitter blow to the delicate plant of artistic appreciation which Charles and his friends had nurtured; and the Puritan revolution, with all its implications, may be said to have disturbed the course of English culture. It had occurred at a vital moment, when a strong feeling for painting was current. Such a magnificent array of paintings was never again to be gathered in England and the wars also served to disperse the collection of the Earl of Arundel. Naturally enough, Charles II, on his return to England, made every effort to reassemble his father's collection, though much was lost irretrievably. The recovery of the collection was entrusted to a Royal Commission, who employed such devious methods as informers to ascertain the whereabouts of many works. But Charles was lucky enough to receive the collection of the Van Reynst brothers, who had bought at his father's sale, as a present from the Dutch Government, and these pictures included the notable portrait of Isabella d'Este (Page 107), now attributed to Giulio Romano. Charles' own passion as a collector lay in other, more terrestrial, directions than his father, and a confirmation of his particular taste lay in the arrival of the Windsor Beauties in the collection. Lely's *Lady Byron* (Page 108), is a luscious comment on the generous pleasures of the Restoration, and a fitting accompaniment to the poems of Rochester, Suckling, and the other wits. This phase in the history of the collections is still not altogether elucidated, and it may well be during Charles II's reign that the famous sketch books by Leonardo da Vinci became the property of the Crown. Yet as a whole there was, after the glorious period of Charles I, a diminution in the character of the Royal collecting and patronage.

William III, for instance, was not the man to mould the arts to reflect his personality: he may have fought Louis XIV, but he was neither his rival in taste nor in artistic feeling. Though Horace Walpole went too far when he said of him that he "contributed nothing to the arts", his patronage was perfunctory rather than passionate. He certainly cared for gardening, and both he and the Queen were interested in the interior decoration of their residences. One may even say that except for the regulation number of portraits, few pictures of distinction entered the collection until the arrival of Frederick, Prince of Wales. He not only encouraged a number of living painters, but was interested in the possessions of the Crown. "I have something of every kind," he told George Vertue, "because I love the arts and curious things." His own taste lay in the direction of the seventeenth century, and he acquired such remarkable paintings as Rubens' *The Gerbier Family* (Page 110), and Van Dyck's double portrait of *Carew and Killigrew* (Page 109). But he was equally attracted by French and Italian painting of the seventeenth century, and secured Claude landscapes, classical compositions by Guido Reni, and the famous volume of sketches by Poussin, which had belonged to Dr. Richard Mead, the friend of Watteau, and earlier to Cardinal Massimi. In other words, Frederick shared the taste of the connoisseurs of his period, which were enshrined in the lectures of Sir Joshua Reynolds, and which appear in the many notable private collections of that epoch.

In the eighteenth century the bridge between the Crown and contemporary painting, which had existed so triumphantly under Charles I, was once more established. The foundation of the Royal Academy, for instance, dates from the reign of George III. Indeed, the emergence of a talented group of portrait painters made such a relationship not only necessary but logical. The King himself was especially interested in Zoffany, Gainsborough and Ramsay, all of whom painted various members of the Royal family, while the patronage of Reynolds was mainly left to the Prince Regent. George III's particular feeling for painting may be seen in his friendship for the American artist Benjamin West, who succeeded Reynolds as President of the Royal Academy. His historical paintings of classical and medieval subjects were designed for the rooms at Buckingham Palace and Windsor Castle, and were typical of the neo-classical historical style at the close of the eighteenth century. Once again, the taste of the times may be seen reflected in the Royal collection, though one may regret the absence of a painter such as Richard Wilson.

Like Charles I before him, George III, whose interest in art had been stimulated by Lord Bute, was well served by his agents. In the early years of his reign he was able to add the most interesting collection of works to have entered the Crown's possession since the time of the Mantuan purchase. His good fortune was due to the taste of Joseph Smith, the British Consul in Venice, who lived in style in a fine palace on the Grand Canal and also owned a villa at Mogliano. Smith spent much of his time in forming his collection of paintings, drawings and books, much of which found their way into the Royal collection. He appears to have been a shrewd, talented man of business and acted as almost the exclusive agent of such contemporary Venetian artists as Sebastiano and Marco Ricci. But it was above all as the business manager of Canaletto that he exerted such a distinct influence, facilitating his contacts with English visitors, and probably arranging his journey to London. His own collection of Canaletto embraced nearly all the master's periods and the fifty-three paintings and over a hundred drawings acquired by George, most of which are still in the Royal collection, provide a full picture of the Venetian artist's merits, from his most romantic views of his own city to his London scenes. The King, or, rather, his agent, Richard Dalton, the librarian of the Royal library, also secured from Smith the interesting collection of drawings and prints belonging to Cardinal Alessandro Albani, with its Carracci's and Domenichino's, which likewise had passed through Smith's hands. Smith's own collection was not only rich in Venetian art, but included such masterpieces as Vermeer's *Lady at the Virginals,* then attributed to Mieris.

George III succeeded in acquiring a remarkable series of works which broaden the scope of the collection, but his taste had neither the sureness nor the personal nature of his son. Pleasure-loving, easygoing, sensitive, George IV had a sense of style and a gusto which found its most lasting monument in the Pavilion. He was, the Duke of Wellington shrewdly noted, "the most extraordinary compound of talent, wit, buffoonery, obstinacy and good feeling—in short a medley of the most opposite qualities, with a great preponderance of good—that I ever saw in any character in my life". Of his character as a man and ruler we have no concern, but what cannot be denied, even by his most censorious opponents, is that he was a fine judge of furniture and painting and that he had a brilliant sense of interior decoration. One feels that George, if he had not sat upon the throne, might, in another age, have made a fortune as a decorator. His own feeling for life and his capacity for pleasure together created a style which is one of the most personal and authentic in English art. Living at a time when some of the most splendid collections on the Continent had been dispersed, George was ably advised by such connoisseurs as the third Lord Hertford and by Benoit, who had been *pâtissier* to Louis XVI, and he bought wisely and well. His buying was not done indiscriminately but with care and taste, and each object was carefully discussed with Lord Hertford before a decision was taken. He took good care, too, to be informed as to the best pictures available, either here or abroad. He had shown an interest in the Dutch school before the Regency and in 1814 acquired the splendid

DAVID GARRICK
Sir Joshua Reynolds, 1723–1792
Collection the Prince Regent
Windsor Castle

PORTRAIT OF A YOUNG LADY
Rubens: Windsor Castle

MRS ROBINSON
Thomas Gainsborough, 1727–1788]
Collection the Prince of Wales
Windsor Castle

A LADY AT THE VIRGINALS
Johannes Vermeer, 1632–1675
Collection George III
Buckingham Palace

A LADY AT A WINDOW WITH A FAN
Rembrandt, 1606–1669
Collection the Prince Regent
Buckingham Palace

THE LETTER
Gerard Ter Borch, 1617–1681
Collection the Prince Regent
Buckingham Palace

A WATERMILL BY A WOODY LANE
Meindert Hobbema, 1638–1709
Collection the Prince Regent
Buckingham Palace

THE NEGRO PAGE
Aelbert Cuyp, 1620–1691
Collection the Prince Regent
Buckingham Palace

THE YOUNG GAMBLERS
Mathieu le Nain, c. 1607–1677
Collection the Prince Regent
Buckingham Palace

Right: The Tribuna, by Johann Zoffany, 1733–1810. Purchased by Queen Charlotte: Windsor Castle

Left: The Archduke Charles by Sir Thomas Lawrence, 1769–1830. Collection the Prince Regent: Windsor Castle

The Prince of Wales's Phaeton and Thomas, the State Coachman, with a pair of Black Horses, a Stable-boy and a Fox Dog, George Stubbs, 1724–1806. Collection George IV: Windsor Castle

THE PRINCE OF WALES AND THE DUKE OF YORK AT PLAY
JOHANN ZOFFANY, 1733–1810
Windsor Castle   Painted for George III

Left: King George III
by Zoffany, Windsor
Castle. Right: Murano
by Canaletto, 1697–
1768, Windsor Castle.
Acquired by George III

ANNIBALE CARRACCI, 1560–1609
Hampton Court Palace

THE TRIUMPH OF TRUTH
Collection of Queen Victoria.

SIR PETER PAUL RUBENS, 1577–1640
Buckingham Palace

THE FARM AT LAEKEN
Collection of George IV

THOMAS ROWLANDSON
Royal Library, Windsor Castle
THE FRENCH REVIEW

collection of Sir Thomas Baring with its wonderful pictures by Terborch, Metsu and Steen. With his particular temperament it was understandable that he should have been attracted by the finish of the Dutch school, and equally so that he had an eye for the merits of Rubens, whose *Farm at Laeken* (Page 121) entered the collection through him. His other acquisitions included Claude's *Europa* (Page 106) and Le Nain's *Gamblers* (Page 117), which was then attributed to Caravaggio and was purchased in public auction. It was George's admiration for the Dutch school which assisted in his appreciation of Wilkie, and he owned some of his finest paintings. Personal taste again accounts for the various sporting pictures that he purchased, as befitted the friend of pugilists and the lover of the turf, and George Stubbs (Page 118) is seen to particular advantage in the collection. For all his faults, and they were very human, George had a sense for art—he admired Jane Austen—and for history, and his commission to Sir Thomas Lawrence to celebrate the downfall of Napoleon by painting the portraits of the chief actors in the allied cause was highly imaginative, though the suggestion did not originate with him. And the Waterloo Chamber must be included with Carlton House and the Pavilion amongst the artistic triumphs of his reign.

One of the results of the sales of the early part of the nineteenth century and the progress of historical knowledge was to direct attention to early periods of Italian art and to the question of attributions. The influence of these factors may be seen in the contribution made by the Prince Consort to the collection. Under the guidance of his adviser, Gruner,

Queen Victoria, the Prince Consort and the Princess Royal at Windsor.
Painted for Queen Victoria by Sir Edwin Landseer (1802–1873).
Windsor Castle

Triptych by Duccio, 1278–1318. Purchased by Prince Albert, 1846. On loan to the National
Gallery from Buckingham Palace

he started to collect early Italian primitives and showed his sense of public duty in purchasing the collection of his cousin, the Prince Oettingen-Wallerstein, which had been exhibited at Kensington Palace with the hope that the nation might acquire it. This collection strengthened the representation of earlier periods in the collection, and included such paintings as the Madonna now given to the Master of the Lucy Legend.

The Prince Consort, together with the Queen, later purchased such important paintings as the Duccio Triptytch (Page 123) and the Montefeltro group by Joos van Wassenhove (below), while other works acquired by the Prince were presented after his death to the National Gallery. His interest in earlier schools was marked. The taste of the Prince and Queen Victoria was not so happy with modern art, and Winterhalter and Landseer were chosen to paint the members of the Royal family. Yet without the inspiration of the Prince Consort, who fully realized the importance of the fine arts in education, the collection would be virtually without the presence of early Italian art.

The collection has not remained static in recent times, and Her Majesty the Queen Mother, whose collecting has lain in other directions, has added a number of paintings of historical importance. Nor have more recent periods been neglected, and Queen Elizabeth has acquired examples of Monet, Sickert and John Piper. As one looks at the Royal pictures down the centuries, one is not only aware of a panorama of history and of the splendours that decorate the palaces, but of the continuity of a tradition. This tradition can never be forgotten. It is the reflection of a sure belief in the standards of civilised life and the realisation that the work of art must and indeed does play an important part in our daily life.

Federico da Montefeltro, 1st Duke of Urbino, by Joos van Wassenhove
(c. 1460–1485). Bought by Queen Victoria. Windsor Castle

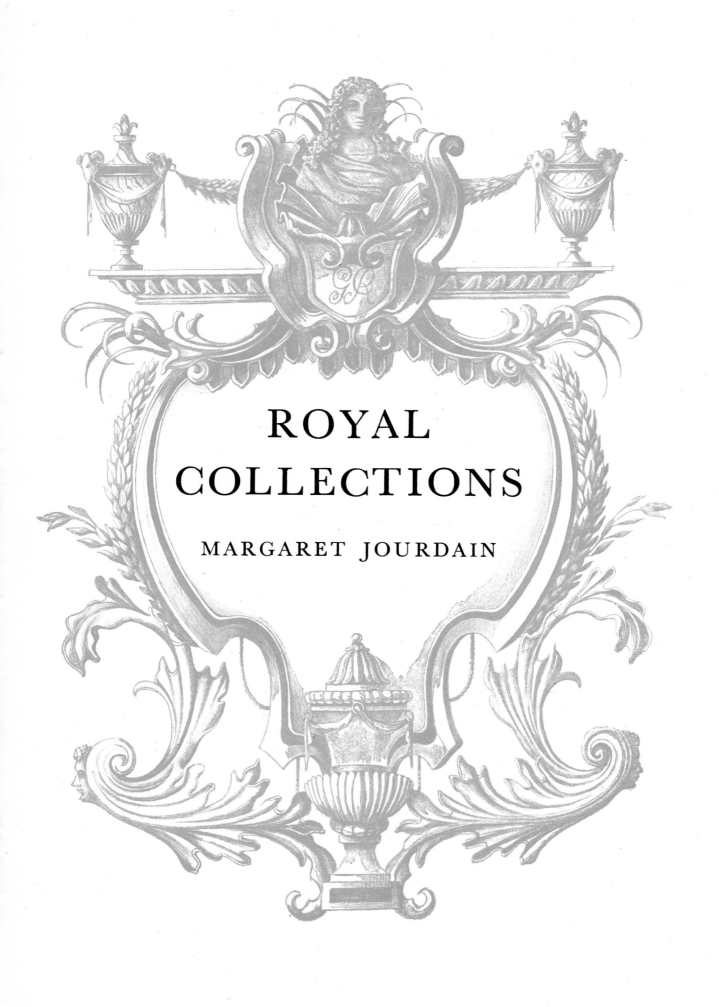

ROYAL
COLLECTIONS

MARGARET JOURDAIN

An urn, a cup, a mug, commemorate the Jubilee of George III

Fig. 11   A panel of Brussels Tapestry   Windsor Castle

ROYAL COLLECTIONS

MARGARET JOURDAIN

THE COLLECTION of furniture in the Royal palaces has fluctuated considerably. There was a complete and immense dispersal after the death of Charles I when the Royal possessions were sold by auction.[1]

A study of the inventories of the palaces and of the Royal tradesmen's accounts give some measure of these losses. At Windsor Castle there are the remains of three splendid sets of tables, stands and mirrors, but only two of the tables and one pair of stands remain. There is no record of the disappearance of the organ case supplied in 1766 by John Bradburn, which he describes as a "very grand organ case, carved with nine varieties of ornaments, viz. satyr boys, musical instruments, drapery for curtains, palms, festoons and husks" in which the carving alone cost one hundred and fifty-six pounds.

During the last four reigns, however, several pieces have made a return journey to the Royal collection: among these is a pair of cabinets bearing Henrietta Maria's monogram (Fig. 1) and given by her to her secretary, confidential adviser and friend, Henry Jermyn, Lord St. Albans,[2] "a prudent old courtier, who was much enriched since her majesty's return in

[1] Later, there was the disappearance of outmoded pieces to make way for new purchases, and the Lord Chamberlain's perquisites.

[2] He directed that these cabinets should be moved from his house in St. James's Square to Rushbrooke, in Suffolk, where they remained until 1910.

Fig. 3. Marquetried bureau with the monogram of William III in the Charles II dining-room, Windsor Castle

Fig. 1. Cabinet dating from the Restoration, bearing the monogram of Henrietta Maria. Van Dyck Room, Windsor Castle

Marquetried cabinet, *circa* 1690, in the Charles II dining-room, Windsor Castle

1660." The cabinets, veneered with oyster pieces of lignum vitae and mounted with escutcheons and small plaques of silver, must date from the Restoration (when Henrietta Maria was provided with a generous income and Somerset House as a residence) and her return to her own country in 1665. The quality of these mounts is in advance of any metal-mounted furniture of the first decade of Charles II's reign. The Flemish cabinet (Fig. 2), overlaid with ebony, ivory and tortoiseshell, encloses small carvings in ivory centring in a figure of James II enthroned under a canopy and supported by figures emblematic of strength and wisdom. This group is flanked by rostral columns, and surmounted by a group of St. George and the Dragon, and a *putto* riding a dolphin—an allusion to the King's lively interest in the navy.[1] As Duke of York he was appointed Lord High Admiral at the Restoration, and continued in that office until 1674.

A table with carved and gilt frame is so closely related to tables and stands at Windsor Castle that it must have been the work of one of the Royal cabinet-makers. The scagliola top centres in the cypher of Queen Anne, surmounted by a Royal crown. This table, which

[1] He regained the powers, if not the full dignity of the Admiralty in 1684. "His seamanship was by no means titular, but shows itself in much of his correspondence with Dartmouth and others." *Dictionary of National Biography*.

Japanese cabinet on a carved base of English workmanship, 18th cent., Queen's Audience Chamber, Windsor Castle

The interior of James II's cabinet (below), containing ivory carvings representing James II enthroned

was given by Queen Anne to Lord Trevor of Bromham, was purchased for the Royal collection in 1938.

The inventory of Charles I's furniture, hangings, pictures, plate and jewels, took a year to complete, and the collection was scattered, the greater portion being purchased by foreigners. At the Restoration, his son returned to empty palaces. In this reign the galleries were refurnished with veneered and marquetried furniture by the Royal cabinet-makers; and the quantity of furniture supplied in William III's reign was large. Of this grand total, dating from about forty years, only a small residue survives. The silver-plated set of table, mirror and stands given to Charles II by the citizens of London was protected from decay by its metal casing. In the table, dating from William III's reign, little woodwork is used, the piece being almost entirely of silver. These silver pieces were concentrated in the drawing-room at Windsor Castle, where Celia Fiennes noted "a large branch of silver, and ye sconces round ye roome of silver, silver table and stands and glass frames".

The metal marquetry of William III's desk-table (Fig. 3) and Queen Mary's cabinet (Fig. 4) has also preserved them intact and unrestored. The desk-table, which bears on an ebony plaque the cypher of William III, has been identified with the "fine writing desk inlaid with metal", supplied by Gerreit Jensen, in 1695, the only cabinet-maker working in the difficult technique

Fig. 2. James II's Cabinet, containing ivory carvings representing James II enthroned, in the Grand Corridor, Windsor Castle

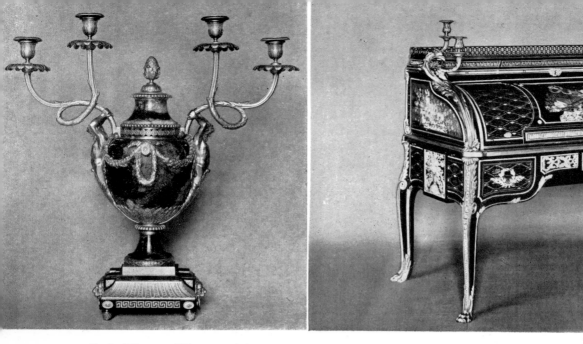

Left: Fig. 15. Vase-candelabra, mounted with ormolu and one of a pair by Matthew Boulton, in the Queen's sitting-room, Windsor Castle. Right: Fig. 7. Cylinder-fronted bureau, one of the finest pieces of French furniture in the Royal collection. In the White drawing-room, Buckingham Palace

of metal marquetry developed in France by André Charles Boulle.

Queen Mary's cabinet (Fig. 4) is an elaborate piece which antedates the Revolution in 1688 and may have been brought to England by the Queen. Its carcase is of rosewood overlaid with geometrical marquetry in brass, white metal, tortoiseshell and ivory, and set with small panels and bosses of lapis lazuli, agate, cornelian and other hard stones. In the centre of the upper stage is a cupboard enclosing a miniature temple seen in perspective, a favourite device of Flemish cabinet-makers. The urns and cresting above the pediment and the caryatid *putti* are gilt. This piece can be seen in a view of the Queen's bedchamber at Kensington Palace in Pyne's *Royal Residences* (1819). Two pieces of marquetry in wood, made by Gerreit Jensen and identified by entries in the Royal wardrobe accounts, survive (Figs. 3 and 4), but in a much restored condition. The writing-table, surmounted by an independent case of small drawers, closely follows contemporary French models. The marquetry of both the writing-table and cabinet is of intricate scroll type. The small drawers in the centre of the separate chest of drawers are fitted for writing. This writing-table is shown in *Royal Residences*, in the King's closet at Kensington, where it is described as "a cabinet curiously inlaid", which is "the more estimable for having been the writing desk of King William III".

Fig. 4. Queen Mary's cabinet, an elaborate piece which antedates the Revolution in 1688

Left: Fig. 6. Louis XV commode in black lacquer, with scroll-work by Jacques Caffieri, in the Picture Gallery, Windsor Castle. Right: A satin-wood commode from Buckingham Palace

There was a renewal of furnishing activity in the reign of George I, and from this period date the gilt table and stands at Hampton Court Palace bearing both the King's cypher and the name of the Royal cabinet-maker and glass-seller, James Moore, a designer of "considerable originality, out of touch with contemporary fashions".

George III spent lavishly on furniture in the first years of his reign, employing, between 1760 and 1764, the brilliant craftsman, William Vile, who had worked for him when Prince of Wales. His work combines a rich exuberance of ornament and the highest finish. Among pieces by this maker at Buckingham Palace are a secretaire with a fretwork superstructure centring in a Royal crown, made for Queen Charlotte in 1761, and bookcase of the Corinthian order made for her in the following year. The cylinder-fronted bureau dates from the clouded years of his reign when he made a brief recovery from his mental breakdown in 1788. The cylinder fall is inlaid with oval medallions of sprays of fruit, and an equestrian portrait of the King, framed in parquetry. The cypher G.R. is inlaid in two places.

The purchases of George as Prince of Wales and King George IV (part of those "great expenses lavished upon art which undermined his popularity") bulk largely in the Royal collection. His redecoration of Carlton House (when the magnificent work by Henry Holland was

Fig. 5. *Armoire* veneered with ebony, inlaid with brass, by André Charles Boulle, in the Grand Corridor, Windsor Castle

still fresh) was considered by a visitor as in "a most extensive and motley taste", and his bias towards Chinese art and decoration was held up to public merriment in the political satires of the day. As late as 1907 a writer speaks of the Royal collection as "only too rich in furniture in the Chinese style", and the amount of this latest interpretation of Oriental art from Carlton House and the Brighton Pavilion is considerable. His purchase of French furniture and porcelain were also of the highest importance. He "bought royally, lavishly", under the guidance of Lord Yarmouth (afterwards Lord Hertford), in whom "he placed well-merited and implicit faith". He had a "genuine but unstable interest in artistic matters".[1]

With the havoc and dispersal of the Royal collections of household goods during the French Revolution, fine French furniture was advantageously purchased by George IV's agents. Two *armoires* by André Charles Boulle in the Grand Corridor at Windsor Castle show the style at its monumental best (Fig. 5). The *armoire* is veneered with ebony, inlaid with lines of brass. The panels of the doors and sides are of tortoiseshell veneer, inlaid with trophies and scrollwork in engraved brass. In the centre of each is a plinth enclosing a small plaque of tortoiseshell stained blue, supporting reliefs in cast and chased ormolu, of Apollo and Daphne and the flaying of Marsyas (after Antoine Coysevox). There is a closely similar *armoire* having the same mounts in the Wallace Collection. The workmanship of these mounts and the foliated hinges is remarkable.[2]

The commode with panels of black lacquer mounted and framed in ormolu bears the mark of the Parisian *ébéniste* who stamped his work with the mark B.V.R.B., and who was sensible of the effective contrast between the mounts and the panels of black lacquer (Fig. 6).

The secretaire, dating from the early years of Louis XVI's reign, is veneered with parquetry and marquetry of woods in which tulipwood and kingwood predominate. In the centre of the front is a large panel inlaid with the Royal arms of France, surrounded by orders of the Golden Fleece and the *Saint Esprit*. Its maker, François Gaspard Teuné, specialised in cylinder-fronted bureaux. One of the finest pieces of French furniture in the Royal collection is a cylinder-fronted bureau in the White Drawing-room at Buckingham Palace (Fig. 7). The back and cylinder fall are overlaid with a rosetted trellis, framing marquetried panels of flowers; the legs are edged with bands of ormolu, which, at the desk height, branch out into candle-branches.[3]

There is a very large collection of clocks in the Royal Palaces, and in Buckingham Palace alone there are upwards of three hundred.

At Buckingham Palace there are two long case clocks with a twelve-month movement, by Tompion, the first dating from about 1695, the second, made by Tompion and Banger between 1702 and 1707. The bulk of the Royal collection, however, dates from the reign of George III and George IV. George III was a generous patron of contemporary clockmakers such as Alexander Cumming, Christopher Pinchbeck and Eardley Norton. The long case astronomical clock by Julien le Roy (1686–1759), an inventive French clockmaker and author of several works on horology (Fig. 8), appears in the background of a group by Zoffany of Queen Charlotte seated at her dressing-table in the "Queen's House" with the

[1] D. Stroud *Henry Holland* (1950), p. 21.
[2] This *armoire* was bought in 1828 for the Royal collection. It was sold in the early years of the nineteenth century at a sale of the suplus furniture.
[3] Illustrated in H. Clifford Smith, *Buckingham Palace*, fig 153.

Vase and cover of
Sèvres porcelain
from Buckingham
Palace

Fig. 9. Four-sided astronomical clock (1768), designed
by George III and Sir William
Chambers

Fig. 13. Vase and
cover of Sèvres
porcelain (1772),
painted by Dodin

Sexagonal vase
from the Royal
Pavilion, Brighton,
now in Windsor
Castle

Below: Drinking
glass said to have
belonged to
Queen Elizabeth

Fig. 10. Clock and barometer of porcelain and ormolu
in the Chinese taste. From the Banqueting Room in the
Royal Pavilion, Brighton, now in the Grand Reception
Room, Windsor Castle

Below: Fig. 14. A *seau* of Sèvres porcelain (part of a
dinner service bearing date marks between 1703 and
1792)

Sexagonal vase
from the Royal
Pavilion, Brighton.
Now in Windsor
Castle

Below: Fig. 15.
The Goodwood
Cup, by Paul Storr
(1830–31)

young Prince of Wales and the Duke of York.[1] Its movement, according to the inscription, was invented by its maker in 1736, and tells solar and mean time and the day of the month. The case is mounted with ormolu and surmounted by a figure of Time.

The design of a clock by the younger Christopher Pinchbeck, in 1768, is attributed in part to George III, and in part to Sir William Chambers; but the graceful detail suggests that the taste of the King's architect predominated in the design of the case of tortoiseshell, mounted with ormolu.[2] This four-sided clock has four dials, one showing the tides at the leading ports of Great Britain, another the signs of the zodiac, a third a planetarium (Fig. 9).

In some clock cases in the Chinese taste, porcelain and ormolu is brilliantly combined. In the case of a clock and barometer made for the Brighton Pavilion, the features and dress of the supporting Chinese figures are carefully rendered (Fig. 10).[3]

The tapestries have a wide range of date. The two Brussels panels which are hung in the Throne Room at Hampton Court Palace are the "oldest examples of applied decorative art that today exist at Windsor Castle".[4] They are woven with an admixture of gold and silver thread, which has darkened and lost its lustre. In one panel the design centres in a double-tiered fountain capped by a cupola wreathed with vines; in the uppermost section of the field, fantastic figures of men and centaurs are introduced, and in the lowest is a procession of animals, panthers, asses and dromedaries, with satyrs. This panel bears the Brussels crown and B. A second panel (which bears no mark) is similar in style and has the same border, is divided into three tiers, and woven with the story of Hercules. Both panels date from the last years of the sixteenth century. A later panel of Brussels tapestry (Fig. 11) bearing the arms of William III and Queen Mary, flanked by figures of Mars and Minerva holding up the Royal crown, is part of a set woven with an admixture of gold and silver thread by the master-weavers de Clerck, Van der Borcht, Cobus and Coenot. There are two panels of their effective design at Windsor Castle.[5] French tapestry of the eighteenth century is represented by two sets woven at the Gobelins, after cartoons by Jean-François Troy, Director of the French Academy at Rome, by the weavers Cozette and Audran. There are six panels from the complete set of the History of Jason (Fig. 12) and seven of the Story of Esther, and both sets are enclosed in frame-pattern borders and in the upper borders are the arms of France. There is a nobility of conception and wide range of colour in these compositions, which recall the work of Le Brun "while in addition there is a certain Italianate ease and lack of restraint".

The collection of Sèvres porcelain was begun by George III, and "a few pieces of Sèvres" were noted by Horace Walpole on his visit to the Queen's House in St. James Park in 1783, but the major part was contributed by George IV. The bills for many of the pieces of Sèvres porcelain purchased by the latter spread over about five years between 1810 and 1815. Of the great collection a vase and cover (Fig. 13), and a *seau* (Fig. 14) are shown. The ground of the vase is a rich *bleu du roi*, and the principal subject, painted by the artist Dodin, is Mercury reading to Venus and Cupid. The panel on the reverse side is painted with a

[1] Painted about 1767.
[2] "The design partly His Majesty's, partly Mr. Chambers's his architect." *Letters and Journal of Lady Mary Coke*, Vol. 2, p. 180–81.
[3] By B. L. Vulliamy, bought in 1809.
[4] G. F. Laking, *Furniture at Windsor Castle*, p. 91
[5] These panels were acquired for the Royal collection in 1914.

Fig. 12. Gobelin tapestry, one of six panels woven with the History of Jason, in the Grand Reception Room, Windsor Castle

Left: Fig. 8. Long case astronomical clock by Julien le Roy (1686-1759), in the Grand Corridor, Windsor Castle. Right: A needlework casket of stump work (dated 1670) on a carved and gilt stand, dating from about 1720. Now in the Charles II dining-room, Windsor Castle

A sofa, part of a set, covered in Beauvais tapestry, in the
Grand Reception Room, Windsor Castle

bouquet of flowers. The painted decoration of the *seau* is brilliantly finished and a serious
rival to the art of the miniaturist.

According to a writer on Royal collections of plate in Europe, their vicissitudes would
fill a large chapter in the history of the arts. Great collections were formed only to be melted
down to provide money, or to meet the demands of fashion. Little remains of the plate
bought by Charles II immediately after the Restoration. It was George IV who was "the first
of the Hanoverian line to display any marked interest in collecting plate". It was he who
acquired the silver-gilt rosewater dish (1595–6) and the vase-shaped Jacobean ewer
(1617–18), and he was also a patron of contemporary silversmiths, such as Paul Storr,[1]
who takes pride of place for fine and finished craftsmanship. The King's interest in
racing is commemorated by the Goodwood Cup (Fig. 15) decorated by two panels, one
embossed with a running horse, the other with a group of the gods adjudging the prize.

The Royal encouragement of skilled workmanship in metal work is shown by the purchase
from Matthew Boulton of a pair of vase-candelabra mounted with ormolu (Fig. 15).
George III bought from him "a pair of cassolets, a Tilies, a Venus clock and some other
things", and a pair of cassolets (both mounted in ormolu) and a pair of blue john candelabra
still form the chimney furniture in the Queen's private drawing-room at Windsor Castle.

[1] 1771–1844.

Two carved and gilt
council chairs, made for
George IV, and now in
the Throne Room Buck-
ingham Palace

ROYAL COURT DRESS

Court Dress. From Heideloff's *Gallery of Fashion*, 1797

JAMES LAVER

ROYAL COURT DRESS

JAMES LAVER

COURT DRESS today is something of a curiosity. It is very much a special occasion costume which very few people have the opportunity of seeing. Even the parade of cars which persisted until the middle 'thirties has now, I believe, been abandoned. Therefore it would be true to say that the general public never sees a Court dress at all. It has become one of those costumes, like Diplomatic dress, which persist in the modern world almost on sufferance; yet Court dress has played a very considerable part in the general history of clothes, and its evolution during the last five or six hundred years cannot fail to be of interest.

Of course, Court costume has a very ancient history. To go no further back than the Byzantine Empire, it would probably be admitted by most scholars that a considerable number of what we now know as ecclesiastical vestments were originally derived from the Court dress of that period. This is a question for specialists. What we are interested in at the moment is the development of Court costume since the rise of the medieval monarchies of Western Europe. We shall get some notion of the importance of the question if we realise that what we know as fashion is a comparatively modern invention, and that it all arose in the luxurious Courts of France and Burgundy during the latter half of the fourteenth century.

For almost a thousand years men's clothes, and even more particularly women's clothes, had few or none of the elements which we should now call fashion. Women wore shapeless, flowing garments and ample veils which concealed their hair entirely and a considerable part of their face. Then suddenly the whole apparatus of fashion was invented in a single generation. Dresses, by means of buckram stiffening, were shaped to the figure. Décolletage made its appearance. The veils on women's heads began to assume all kinds of fantastic forms. What is even more interesting to note is the way in which women for a hundred and fifty years continued to wear a veil, yet deliberately turned it into an instrument of attraction. It would be almost true to say that except for the exposed legs of the nineteen-twenties, fashion has invented nothing new.

For many years after this, Court dress was not a variety of ordinary fashionable dress. On the contrary, ordinary fashionable dress was a modification of Court dress, less *outré*, less daring, and slightly less elaborate. Court dress, in short, was simply the grandest clothes of the period. In the presence of the king, the ladies of the Court made themselves as attractive as possible, while indicating at the same time the richness of their own or their husband's estates. Men's Court dress was intended to show the wealth of its wearers, as when the great Duke of Buckingham appeared at Court with a hundred thousand pounds' worth of jewels sewn all over his doublet.

Louis XIV of France was one of the greatest sticklers for the elaboration of Court dress, and especially insisted on décolletage, even, strange as it may seem, when the Court was attending Mass. He would even go about among the congregation and turn out the ladies, however old and skinny, who were not décolleté to the degree which he thought pleasing to God because it was so pleasing to himself. Throughout the eighteenth century, Court ladies wore contemporary dress, and so of course did the men, whose embroidered coats at Versailles or St. James's were only slightly more elaborate than could be seen in the fashionable haunts of Paris and London.

It was not until the end of the eighteenth century that a divergence began to make itself felt between fashionable costume and Court dress. This was due in England to the strange persistence of the hoop. Earlier in the century hoops had been worn by every woman with any claims to fashion, but about the time of the French Revolution ordinary clothes, even fashionable ones, became comparatively plain, and abandoned the hoop altogether. The hoop, however, persisted at Court with some strange results, as can be seen very plainly from our illustrations.

It was at this time, too, that Court dress, especially for women, may be said to have stereotyped itself. Plumes in the hair were worn by every fashionable woman in the seventeen-nineties: they have persisted in Court dress ever since; so have the long white gloves which came in with the new short-sleeved gowns. This is in line with the inevitable tendency to formalise itself which is shown by all official costume.

This tendency to carry over elements from an older costume is seen most strikingly in the early years of the nineteenth century. Shortly before the year 1800 women's waists left their natural position and ascended to under the armpits. This was in its way a very attractive fashion, but when a woman went to Court she was compelled to put on hoops. The result was ludicrous; the sudden swelling of the skirt started much too high up for any grace or convenience; indeed it might be said that a woman's hips were now on a level with her bust. At last Prinny, afterwards George IV, who at least had an eye for the elegance of a figure, abolished this absurd custom. Hoops, of course, returned to Court dress in the late eighteen-fifties, but only because by now the crinoline was part of ordinary fashionable dress.

Indeed, we can say that from this moment when hoops were abolished, Court dress has been ordinary fashionable dress, only slightly grander and provided with a train, and, of course, with the addition of plumes in the hair and the inevitable long white gloves. Perhaps the limit was reached in the second half of the 'eighties. It can be seen quite plainly in contemporary numbers of magazines like *The Queen*. For the Drawing Room held on

Court Dresses. From Heideloff's *Gallery of Fashion*, 1801, 1797, 1795

Lady and Gentleman in Court Dress. From *Le Beau Monde*, 1806–1807

Court Dress. From *La Belle Assemblée*, 1817

Court Dress, 1801

Bottom left: Court Dress. From *La Belle Assemblée*, 1832
Bottom centre and right: Court Dresses. From Heideloff's *Gallery of Fashion*, 1796, 1801

March 23rd, 1886, *The Queen* gives a double-spread illustrating five of the most elaborate toilettes. In each case the train was between twelve and fifteen feet long. One of the toilettes is described as follows: "Train of dark and light grey velvet brocade, handsomely trimmed on one side with Irish lace and bunches of feathers. The petticoat consists of a lovely piece of Irish lace mounted on satin and draped with feathers." The lady in question not only wore ostrich plumes on her head but no less than seven great bunches of them elsewhere.

A certain poetry still clings about the descriptions of dresses of former ages. Another toilette is described as follows: "An elegant train of golden *feuille morte* brocade trimmed with Brussels lace; a petticoat of *feuille morte Duchesse* satin was draped with lace and one side was entirely embroidered with beads. The bodice which matched the train was trimmed with feathers and lace; diamond ornaments were worn."

Such extreme elaboration in Court attire persisted almost until the outbreak of the First World War, although it is true that the designers of the year 1910–11 had some difficulty in reconciling the hobble skirt of the period with the long Court train.

After the War there was such a drastic simplification in ordinary evening dress for women that it could not help being reflected, to some extent, even in the costumes worn at Their Majesties' Courts. But if the train was an absurdity when worn with a hobble skirt, it was even more so when joined to the knee-length skirts of the middle 'twenties. Plumes in the hair, a long train behind and a skirt down to the knees in front was a true Hottentot mode. If people had not been completely blinded (as they always are) by contemporary fashion, they would have seen how ridiculous such a costume was and must be.

Greater elegance was possible once long skirts for the evening had returned, and some very elegant neo-classical models were produced in the early 'thirties. Today we can say that contemporary fashion blends itself very happily with those formal additions which go to make up Court dress. The principle of a completely different dress for Court wear has been almost universally abandoned. In other words, women want to wear their Court dress again as ordinary evening dress, so are kept very strictly within the limitations of the prevailing mode. One can only regret that the modern world has so completely deprived us of a platform for any kind of finery, that comparatively few people benefit either by seeing or wearing the more elaborate creations of the couturier's art, for women's Court dress today is as

Queen Victoria, in spite of her small stature, always had the dignity of a Queen

QUEEN ALEXANDRA
1844–1925

The regal beauty of Queen Alexandra is well shown both when she is wearing Court Dress or Coronation Robes, as in the centre panel of photographs, and in less formal attire

142

A portrait of Queen Alexandra by Alice Hughes

Gernsheim Collection

Her Majesty Queen Mary. Below: In the dress worn at the Coronation of Edward VII, 1902

Dignity and charm have always been combined throughout her life as Princess of Wales, as Queen and as Queen Mother

Right: Her
Majesty Queen
Elizabeth
Cecil Beaton

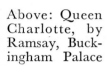

Above: Queen
Charlotte, by
Ramsay, Buck-
ingham Palace

Right: Queen
Charlotte, by
Benjamin West,
Buckingham
Palace. *Repro-
duced by gracious
permission of
H.M. the King*

Left: Lady
Arabella Stuart,
by Gheeraerts
Hampton Court

Below: Prin-
cess Elizabeth,
by an Unknown
Artist, Windsor
Castle. *Repro-
duced by gracious
permission of
H.M. the King*

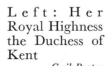

Left: Her
Royal Highness
the Duchess of
Kent
Cecil Beaton

elegant if not as rich as it has ever been, and a great deal easier to wear than in most epochs of the past.

And now let us turn to the much duller subject of men's Court dress. Velvet Court Dress (Old Style, as it is described in the official Handbooks) consisted of a black silk velvet coat with a standing collar, with seven buttons on the right front and seven notched holes on the left—purely vestigial, for the buttons were not intended to button. We have already mentioned the curious tendency of all official costume to stereotype and even to fossilise itself. The cuffs had turn-backs with three notched holes and buttons. The body of the coat was lined with white silk and the skirts with black.

With this went black silk velvet breeches, with three small steel buttons and cut steel buckles at the knees. The hat was a black beaver or silk cocked hat, with a steel loop on a black silk cockade or rosette. There was a lace frill at the throat and ruffles at the wrist, and, of course, a sword.

But the most interesting object in this costume, which is plainly derived from eighteenth century dress, was what is described as a black silk "wig bag" attached to the coat at the back of the neck, hanging over the collar; in short, a feature similar to the flash worn by the Royal Welch Fusiliers. This object, now detached from what it once adorned, is the only relic of the wig worn by the eighteenth-century gentleman.

In the new style velvet Court dress this curious relic is abandoned, as well as the ruffles at wrist and throat. Instead, an evening stiff shirt and white waistcoat, with a white tie, are worn. In practice, even this has been more and more completely dislodged by the *levée* dress, which substitutes dress trousers for breeches. In short, even men's Court dress gradually accommodates itself to contemporary fashion with a time-lag which may be anything up to a hundred and fifty years.

Today, when we are so conscious of the increasing drabness of the world, we should, perhaps, be grateful for any survival of a more picturesque age. It is certainly to be hoped that Court dress, both for men and women, will never pass completely into the limbo of forgotten things.

Queen Charlotte in her Dressing-room, by Zoffany, Windsor Castle. *Reproduced by gracious permission of H.M. the King*

ROYAL GARDENS

MOLLIE SANDS

In the gardens
of Hampton
Court Palace

Alec Murray

ROYAL GARDENS

MOLLIE SANDS

THE LOVE OF GARDENS and of gardening shown so conspicuously by our present Royal family continues a noble tradition. The Royal gardens today—whether private, like Buckingham Palace and Marlborough House, or graciously thrown open to the public like Kensington and Hampton Court—show many signs of the personal interest taken in them by their Royal owners. Indeed, all through English gardening history, royalty has led the way in introducing new ideas of design and cultivation.

MEDIEVAL TIMES

A pleasure garden was a luxury such as only royalty or the wealthiest nobles could afford in medieval times, for in an age of civil strife it was more important to make a home safe than to make it beautiful. Henry III was one of the first English monarchs to spend money on the adornment and domestic comfort of his palaces, and he was censured for his extravagance. In 1250 he ordered the bailiff at Woodstock to make within the Queen's walled garden "a becoming and honourable herbary, in which the same Queen may be able to amuse herself", and in the same year the herbary at Clarendon was repaired and enclosed by a paling. A herbary or arbour in medieval times was a small enclosure where herbs of all kinds were grown for pleasure, for food and for medicine. There you might see roses, sunflowers, saffron, thyme, parsley, lettuce, sage and borage, and probably fruit trees as well—quinces, medlars, peaches and pears. In the centre there would be a pond, which in later years was replaced by a decorative fountain. All such pleasure gardens or herbaries were enclosed by walls, thick hedges or some kind of paling. At first these enclosures were a necessary protection against wild beasts, and later they ensured a privacy rarely enjoyed within doors in medieval living conditions. The herbary was a favourite place for lovers' trysts, or for small parties of ladies and gentlemen to make informal music together, or read aloud from some romance, seated on turfed benches round the wall. A small garden of this kind might be found within the castle itself, while outside the main fortifications there was often a plant yard or orchard (a rudimentary kitchen garden), as well as a larger space for tournaments and games.

Chaucer gives some charming pictures of diminutive fourteenth-century gardens with their green turf

> So small, so thick, so short, so fresh of hew
> That most like to green wool, wot I, it was—

and their enclosing hedge

> . . . as thick as is a castle wall.

It was a Royal garden of this kind that the Scottish King James I saw from

Left: A Rose Hedge in the Castle Battlements. From *The Romaunt of the Rose*

Right: The Moat Garden overlooked by the Norman Tower, Windsor Castle

the window of his prison in the Norman Tower at Windsor early in the fifteenth century:

> Now was there maid fast by the touris wall
> A gardyn faire, and in the corner is set
> Ane herbere grene. . . .

There sang the little sweet nightingale, loud and clear, and there in juniper-shaded alleys walked the golden-haired Lady Joan Beaufort who became his queen. Work on the present moat garden early in this century discovered traces of the old garden and its paths.

Shakespeare sets a famous scene between Richard II's Queen and the gardeners in a now forgotten Royal garden at King's Langley, but he depicts a garden of his own age, with clipped hedges and knot gardens, rather than a medieval herbary. The gardens of Greenwich—much favoured by the Tudors—seem to have been first laid out in the reign of Henry VI, when the estate was known by the charming name of Placentia. Edward IV,

Left: The Grotto of St. George in the Moat Garden, Windsor Castle

Right: The Fountain in the Moat Garden, Windsor Castle

too, must have taken a certain pride in his gardens, for when he received Louis de Bruye at the Tower in 1472 he showed him "his garden and vineyard of pleasure".

THE RENAISSANCE

But it was not until the last decisive battle of the Wars of the Roses had been fought that Kings could give real thought to the peaceful art of gardening. The great age of English Royal gardens begins with the Tudors, or perhaps we should say with the second Tudor. There are records of payments by the careful Henry VII for the upkeep of his gardens; in 1502, for instance, a herber was made for the Queen in the Little Park of Windsor. But lavish expenditure on gardens begins with Henry VIII. The monarchy was now secure, and he made it splendid, a task for which he was admirably fitted by nature and circumstances. He had an appreciation of at least the showier arts of the Italian Renaissance, and he was the absolute king of a country that was beginning to play an important part in Europe.

Perhaps the most splendid of his many homes was the now vanished Nonesuch. In front of the fantastic, Italianate palace lay a formal knot garden, divided into four parterres. Knot gardens came into fashion in early Tudor days; the outlines of a geometrical pattern were planted in some close-growing shrub which was kept clipped, and the design was filled in with small flowers such as daffodils, bachelors' buttons or small hyacinths, or even with coloured sand. Between the parterres stood fountains, sundials and other ornaments of Italian design.

When Henry VIII came into possession of Hampton Court he enlarged Wolsey's pleasure gardens. There were already knot gardens, covered alleys and sweet-scented arbours, what Cavendish called

> My gardens sweet, enclosed with walles strong,
> Embanked with benches to sitt and take my rest
> The knotts so enknotted it cannot be exprest . . .

Henry added a Mount, that essential feature of a fashionable sixteenth- and seventeenth-century garden, crowned by a three-storeyed pavilion, bearing on its leaden cupola a heraldic beast carrying a vane. The winding path which led up to this pavilion was also bordered with heraldic beasts, and yet more beasts stood about the pond in the Pond Garden, all

The Royal Palace of Windsor Castle (from an early engraving): "The Scituation of this charming Castle, seems designed by Nature for Royal Majesty, being on the top of a rising ground which with an August state overlooks all the adjacent country. The building consists of 2 large Courts, with a Tower betwixt them where resides the Governor. In the Upper Court is the Royal Palace and in the middle of ye Square K. Charles 2. a horseback: round the Square without, is the Noblest Terrass in the world"

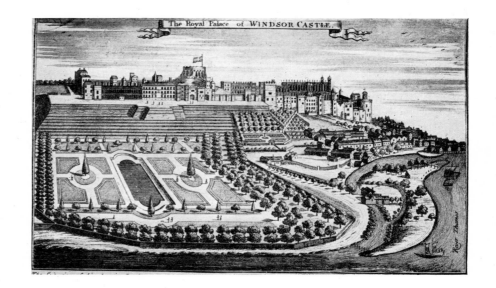

painted in their heraldic colours. He stocked his New Garden with roses, violets, primroses, mint, sweet williams and gillyflowers, and there was fruit in abundance in the orchards. Henry gave his gardener at Hampton Court a special reward for growing melons and cucumbers, notoriously difficult to rear. A piece of ground of about seven acres formed his tiltyard, and accounts of the tournaments held there read like the Field of the Cloth of Gold in minature, so gorgeous was the pageantry.

Of Henry VIII's three children it is Elizabeth we can picture most happily in the Royal gardens. There was an increasing variety of herbs and flowers of all kinds in her reign, and an increased interest in the art of gardening. Her subjects brought back new plants from distant parts of the world, and her poets sang the praises of the flowers they saw around them. Greenwich received her with a splendid piece of floral pageantry in the first year of her reign, when the banqueting house set up in the Park was decorated with birch branches, gillyflowers, lavender and marigolds, the windows filled with plants in pots, and the floor strewn with rushes and herbs. The design of gardens, however, changed little; they were still cut up into small enclosures which gave shelter both against wind and against prying eyes, and there were pleached alleys where you could walk in the worst weather. There were "cabinets of verdure" at Nonesuch, and shady arbours at Hampton Court where Elizabeth held some of her most important interviews. In autumn and winter she walked briskly in Hampton Court Gardens "to catch her a heate", when she thought she was unobserved, but moved "with a sort of grandity" when anyone was looking. Elaborate waterworks which played practical jokes on the bystanders were fashionable. In 1590 she erected in the Clock Court at Hampton Court a fountain which could "make the water play upon the ladies and others who are standing by", and at Nonesuch a pyramid of marble concealed pipes ready to "spurt upon all who come within their reach".

It was in the reign of Elizabeth's successor, James I, that Bacon's essay *On Gardens* was published, which describes the ideal English garden of the sixteenth and seventeenth centuries. James himself—a direct descendant of the James Stuart who was imprisoned at Windsor—is remembered in English gardening history for his championship of the mulberry. He hoped to introduce silk-weaving into this country, and it was for the sake of the silk-worms that he ordered mulberry trees to be planted, and himself set aside a piece of ground near Westminster Palace as a Mulberry Garden. The plan failed, but many a mulberry tree planted in 1609 still remains and bears fruit, gnarled and decrepit though it may appear.

THE FRENCH FASHIONS OF CHARLES II

There was little change from Bacon's conception of garden design for another sixty years or so, but Charles II "made more notable changes, and added more Royal Decorations since the ten years of his happy Restoration than any of his Ancestors ever thought of in the Space of a whole Age". So wrote one of the French gardeners Charles brought over from France to carry out the new ideas he had seen during his exile. These ideas, of which André Le Nôtre was the chief exponent, were more suited to the way of life of the wealthy and absolute Louis XIV than to that of Charles II, whose money was as limited as his power. An English Versailles was far beyond Charles II's means. Yet he achieved a gardening revolution on a small scale.

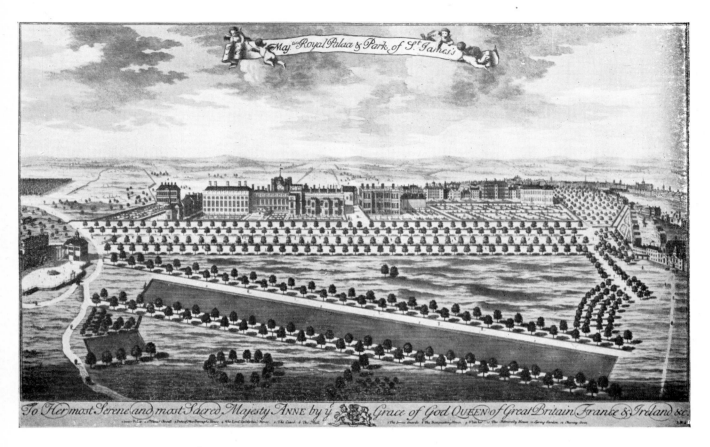

To Her most Serene and most Sacred Majesty ANNE by y᷎ Grace of God QUEEN of Great Britain France & Ireland &c

THE ROYAL PALACE AND PARK OF ST. JAMES'S

Until it was enclosed by Henry VIII, St. James's Park was a huge undrained field belonging to the hospital, afterwards St. James's Palace. Charles II had the Park replanted and beautified according to the fashion and taste of the time. One of Charles's advisers was Le Nôtre, architect of the groves and grottos of Versailles. The Park remained much as Charles planned it during the succeeding reigns of William and Mary and Anne. Pepys refers in his diaries of 1660 to the making of a "river through the Park", and of 300 men, "every day employed in his majesty's worke in making the River in St. James's Park and repairing Whitehall." The mansion at the west end of the canal is Buckingham House, built in 1705 for the Duke of that name. George IV, who finally rearranged the Park much as it is today, had Buckingham House rebuilt from the designs of John Nash in about 1825

Statues in the East Terrace Garden, Windsor Castle

Instead of being divided into many small enclosed plots, the entire ground was now laid out in one large symmetrical design, in which all the features—parterres, covered walks, statues, fountains—were subordinated to the whole. There were artificial sheets of water, cascades and terraces, where the terrain allowed. One of the basic principles of Le Nôtre's designs was to make at least three straight avenues radiate from the centre of the mansion. Long avenues converged on some central point, and the eye travelled along seemingly infinite green vistas to some carefully-placed statue or fountain.

St. James's was laid out on the principles of Le Nôtre in the early days of the Restoration. Several springs and pools of water were united to form a straight canal, running from the Whitehall end nearly to the Chelsea Gate. Right and left of this canal, linked by semicircles of lime trees, avenues branched off to join the Mall, on one side, and Birdcage Walk on the other. The Mall and Birdcage Walk converged on the Chelsea Gate end of the canal. Canal and avenues alike were bordered with lime trees. Nowadays the Mall leads to Buckingham Palace, which in Charles II's day did not exist.

Pepys watched the work at St. James's with great interest. On September 16, 1660, he went to see "how far they had proceeded in the Pell Mell, and in making a river through the Park", and in October he admired "the several engines at work to draw up water". The next summer he commented on "the great variety of fowle" in the Park. Charles kept ducks and other water birds in a decoy, and he had a collection of aviaries along Birdcage Walk. The birdcages have vanished, but there is still a great variety of fowl to be observed in St. James's Park.

The Royal gardens lay between the Palace and the site of the present Admiralty Arch, along the Mall. There were a few houses on the south side of Pall Mall with terrace gardens looking on to the Royal parterres. One day, when Evelyn was walking in these parterres with Charles II, "Mrs. Nellie" looked out of her garden "on a terrace on the top of the wall" and held "a very familiar discourse" with a gentleman whose name Evelyn discreetly indicates by a dash, though his identity is not difficult to guess.

At Hampton Court a canal was dug from the east front of the Palace, and avenues of lime trees planted to radiate each side of it. Charles put in charge of these alterations an English gardener, John Rose, who had studied under Le Nôtre. Rose specialised in growing what were known as "choice greens", i.e. orange trees and other delicate shrubs, but he is most famous for having grown the first pineapple in England. In the illustration on page 159 we see him presenting this prodigy to his master. Other specimens of his "choice greens" in tubs and pots may be seen in the picture.

Windsor was a favourite summer residence of Charles II, and here also formal gardens were laid out, as may be seen from the illustration on page 151, and straight avenues planted, of which the Long Walk is a good example.

DUTCH WILLIAM

William and Mary are generally credited with introducing Dutch fashions into English gardening, but Franco-Dutch is a more correct description, for their Royal gardens in Holland had already been influenced by French ideas. Daniel Marot, the Huguenot pupil of Le Nôtre, worked for William III both in Holland and England. Dutch gardens, however, had modified rather than abandoned the idea of small enclosures, possibly because their

The Great Vine, Hampton Court Palace, planted in 1769

The Sunken Garden, Hampton Court Palace

area was often cut up by water-courses. Arbour walks had windows through which the rest of the garden could be seen, an idea suitably revived in recent years at Kensington in the lime walks round the sunk garden. The *clairvoyée*, or ornamental grille, was used as a kind of barrier through which you could still see a vista. The late seventeenth-century Tijou screens at Hampton Court (see p. 159) are a beautiful example of the *clairvoyée*. Tall trees did not grow well in Holland, because of the high winds, but Dutch gardeners specialised in clipped shrubs and topiary work of all kinds.

The garden at Kensington (bought from Lord Nottingham in 1689) was laid out in a Dutch style by George London and his assistant, Henry Wise. They must have been responsible for a fine specimen of topiary work known as the "Siege of Troy": yews and variegated hollies were cut in imitation of bastions and fortifications. Something similar was created at Hampton Court by the same gentlemen, known as "Troy Town". Both "Troys" have disappeared, but their more famous topiary masterpiece remains: the Maze at Hampton Court.

At Hampton Court the western end of the canal was filled in, and the Great Fountain Garden made; a central fountain was surrounded by twelve smaller fountains, with semicircular parterres laid out in scroll patterns outlined in dwarf box and filled in with powdered stone of red, blue and yellow. Alternate pyramidal yews and round holly bushes edged the gravel paths. These may still be seen, but like Charles II's lime trees, they have outgrown the symmetry of their original forms.

Queen Mary had a genuine love of gardening, and like other gardeners, she had to admit

French fashions of Charles II are shown in this painting of the symmetrical gardens of Hampton Court Palace

The formality of the gardens at Hampton Court Palace. From an early engraving

that her fondness for rare plants "drew an expense after it". Her "exoticks" and her orange trees were kept in the winter in the Orangery at Hampton Court, and in the cloisters of Wren's new quadrangle. But at Kensington the delicate plants were moved in the winter to the Brompton nursery of London and Wise, for there was no orangery at Kensington until the reign of her sister Anne.

This Orangery, or "stately greenhouse", was built by Wren to house Queen Anne's "foreign plants and fine neat greens", and about the same time he built the beautiful alcove, now moved to Marlborough Gate. Queen Anne enlarged the gardens of Kensington by taking in thirty acres to the north, but she parted with the western end of the gardens of St. James's when she leased a piece of land to the Duke and Duchess of Marlborough. Marlborough House, built by Wren, and its grounds were held by the Churchill family until 1817, when they were purchased by the Crown and once more became Royal.

GEORGIAN TIMES

The gayest years at Kensington and Hampton Court were those of the early Georgian age. George I contributed little to this gaiety, but his son and daughter-in-law, George and Caroline, were attended by a group of Maids of Honour as merry as they were decorative, and by the writers and wits of the age. The ladies' gaily coloured, bell-shaped hoops looked like a bed of moving tulips as they swayed along the walks at Kensington. For a time the Lodge in the Little Park at Richmond, east of the present Kew Observatory, became the summer residence of this court, and there also were spacious gardens.

It was Caroline, after she became Queen, who introduced into the Royal Gardens the landscape style. A new interest in the paintings of Claude, Poussin and Salvator Rosa, and

a reaction against the formality of Le Nôtre, led to the abandonment of straight avenues, straight canals and symmetrical arrangements in favour of a deliberate imitation of the irregularity of nature. Charles Bridgeman, employed to remodel Kensington, did not go so far in the pursuit of irregularity as some of his successors. Thus at Kensington he retained the Le Nôtre idea of three converging avenues, but thanks to the sunk fence between the Gardens and Hyde Park there seems no barrier between art and nature. This sunk fence, known as a Ha! Ha! from the surprise which it caused, was Bridgeman's invention, and added greatly to the effect of space and distance. The "Bason" (the Round Pond) was given no fountain, and the sheet of water formed out of six ponds was a Serpentine, not a straight canal. William Kent went farther in his pursuit of the picturesque, and at Kensington he even planted some dead trees. At Hampton Court he replaced the scroll-work by "natural" green turf. But the formal seventeenth-century design was left more or less alone by the various "improvers". Even "Capability" Brown refrained from drastic improvements, and the chief memorial to him at Hampton Court is the Great Vine, planted while he was in charge of the Gardens, in 1769.

Queen Caroline's daughter-in-law, Princess Augusta, founded the Royal garden which has had the greatest influence on

Urn and pedestal in the gardens of Hampton Court Palace

gardens all over the world—Kew. There had been a garden at Kew in the seventeenth century, but when Princess Augusta and her husband went to live there in the early 1730's, they made many improvements. It was not until 1759–60, however, when she was a widow, that she began laying out the Botanic Gardens in earnest, with William Aiton as head gardener and Lord Bute as general "scientific director". Plants and seeds came to Kew from all over the world, and this was almost pioneer work in an age which thought more of "landscape" than of horticulture. Not that "landscape" was neglected, for here William Chambers built some of his most charming garden pavilions, all the more important because the ground at Kew was flat and afforded few natural features of interest. As a Guide of 1770 put it: "The Gardens of Kew are not very large, nor their situation by any means advantageous; as it is low and commands no Prospect". Many of Chambers' buildings have disappeared and nature has modified the settings of those which remain. But that masterpiece of *chinoiserie*, the Pagoda, still offers a pleasing prospect from many parts of the gardens. After Princess Augusta died, her son George III continued to take an interest in Kew, helped by Sir Joseph Banks, and in his reign it was joined to the gardens of Richmond.

It was George III who bought Buckingham House, built early in the eighteenth century on part of James I's Mulberry Garden. The gardens of the original house had a terrace and a little park with the inevitable canal and lime trees. When Nash rebuilt the Palace for George IV—between 1825–37—he turned the canal into an ornamental water, cut down most of the trees, and laid out lawns, thickets and glades in the taste of the time. It was in George IV's reign also that St. James's Park was given something like its present aspect.

Although deserted by the Sovereign, Kensington Gardens remained Royal, and in the 1820's little Princess Victoria could be seen running up and down the Broad Walk, taking the air in her pony carriage, or breakfasting on the lawn in front of the palace. But in later years she spoke of the gardens of Claremont with more affection than those of Kensington.

Above: Princess Augusta founded the Royal garden which has had the greatest influence on gardens all over the world—Kew. Right: A temple in Kew Gardens

157

The Conservatory of the Brighton Pavilion, the West Corridor with the Enfilade increased by a Mirror. From *Designs for the Pavilion at Brighton*, by H. Repton, Esq.

Below, right: "That masterpiece of *chinoiserie*, the Pagoda in the gardens of Kew"

Gardens are Works of Art

"Designs that are vast only by their dimensions, are always the sign of a common and low imagination; no work of art can be great but as it deceives, to be otherwise is the prerogative of nature only." From *Designs for the Pavilion at Brighton*, by H. Repton, Esq., 1808

The Waterloo Vase, Buckingham Palace

Below left: The "Long Walk" at Windsor Castle, with the quadruple avenue of elms three miles long, planted by Charles II

Sun House, Buckingham Palace
Left: Lead Venus. Sunken Garden,
Hampton Court Palace

The Tijou Screen, Hampton Court
Palace

Cleopatra.
The King's
Privy
Garden,
Hampton
Court
Palace

Charles II receiving the first pineapple grown in England from John Rose, the
Royal gardener, at Dawney Court, the seat of the Duchess of Cleveland

Cleopatra.
The King's
Privy
Garden,
Hampton
Court
Palace

Left: A view
of the "Ha-
Ha" and
Mount, 1736
Kensington
Gardens

Right: In
Kensington
Gardens,
near the
Serpentine,
1790

159

Claremont had been bought for Princess Charlotte and her husband, Prince Leopold, and after her tragic death it remained in the possession of Prince Leopold, Queen Victoria's favourite uncle. When she and the Prince Consort stayed there in the early years of their married life, she wrote that the place brought back to her the happiest days of her otherwise dull childhood, and it is said that in those gardens she first sketched from nature.

QUEEN VICTORIA AND HER DESCENDANTS

A new phase in Royal gardens begins with the accession of Queen Victoria. Hampton Court had ceased to be a Royal residence at the death of George II, and in 1838 Queen Victoria threw the gardens open to the public. Kew had fallen into sad decay since 1820—in which year both George III and Sir Joseph Banks died—and in 1840 it was handed over to H.M. Commissioners of Woods and Forests.

Henry VIII, Charles II, William and Mary, Queen Caroline and the Princess Augusta each developed the gardens in which they were most interested according to the fashions of their day. Queen Victoria and the Prince Consort did the same. It was at Osborne they were best able to express their own tastes in garden design, which were those of their age. In the early nineteenth century there was a reaction against "landscape", and a return to a certain amount of formality, with a new element added—colour. Flowers, which had played little part in the formal garden or the landscape garden, came into fashion again. The great improvement in glass-houses led to those displays of carpet-bedding in vividly contrasting colours which were one of the characteristics of the well-to-do Victorian garden. The Italian type of garden with terraces, flights of steps, pergolas and statuary was much admired, and had a dignity of its own where the terrain was suitable. A fine garden of this kind was designed for Osborne by the Prince Consort, assisted by Professor Grüner of Dresden. Much of the tree-planting was supervised by the Royal couple themselves, and their children took charge of the gardens belonging to their play-house, the Swiss Cottage. Each child had a spade, hoe and wheelbarrow, engraved with the owner's initials.

The love of gardening so early implanted was not lost in later life. Prince Arthur, Duke of Connaught, made of Bagshot Park one of the finest of Royal gardens. And the head gardener of Sandringham, writing in 1906, spoke of His Majesty King Edward VII as "the greatest patron horticulture ever had".

Sandringham was to King Edward and Queen Alexandra what Osborne had been to Queen Victoria and the Prince Consort. There they introduced the ideas of late nineteenth-century gardening. Formal carpet-bedding gave place to borders in which grew hardy herbaceous plants, in masses of carefully-blended colour. The herbaceous border, the wild garden, the rock garden and the bog garden were innovations of this period, and all were introduced at Sandringham. The first herbaceous border there was designed by Queen Alexandra herself.

Queen Mary continued this personal interest in the gardens of Sandringham, and other Royal homes. Few Royal ladies have had such a practical knowledge of gardening, and her influence has extended to the London Parks and open spaces. All the Royal family indeed take an interest in this most English of the arts. Their annual visit to the Royal Horticultural Society's show in the grounds of Chelsea Hospital is a reminder not only of their personal interest, but of the part which royalty has played in the development of gardening in England for many centuries.

ROYAL

ALBUM

"The art of Photography is indeed as great a step in the fine arts as the steam engine was in the mechanical arts, it has called to its aid the highest resources of chemistry & Physics" *Times 1842*

The progress made in bringing, we might say to perfection, this surprising discovery must stagger the most incredulous. The fleshy hue and tints, the play of emotion, the glow of breathing life are all embodied. *Times 1842*

Queen Victoria and Prince Albert. A photograph taken by Roger Fenton in 1854

Duchess of Kent, mother of Queen Victoria, 1861

Duchess of Kent with her grandson, Prince Alfred, 1861

Victoria and Albert,
Windsor, March 1st, 1861

The Princess Royal, the Prince of Wales, Princess Alice and Prince Alfred.
Osborne, August, 1853

Princess Louise, March, 1861

The Princess Alice. Osborne,
May 26th, 1857

Princess Beatrice

Princess Beatrice, May, 1868

Princess Louise, April, 1862

Princess Beatrice, March 26th, 1864

Prince Alfred, 1854

*Prince Alfred as Bacchus, Buckingham
Palace Theatricals, 1854*

*The Prince of Wales, February 8th,
1854*

*The Princess Royal and her brother, Buckingham Palace Theatricals,
1854*

The Queen and Princess Louise.
(John Brown holding pony)

The Princess Royal and Prince
Frederick William of Prussia on
their honeymoon. January, 1858

Princess Alice, February, 1861

Princess Louise

The Queen, 1869

Prince Leopold

Prince Leopold

Victoria with Princess Beatrice, 1883

Prince Leopold

The Prince Consort. December, 1861

Left: Mourning Prince Albert, 1862, and (right) at Balmoral on the first sad anniversary

The Widow, 1862

Her Majesty' command photo graph for th Diamond Jubi lee, August 1897

Nice, April, 1895:
Princess Victoria,
Princess Beatrice,
Queen Victoria,
attended by Sheikh
Ghulan Mustafa and
Sheikh Chidda

From left: Princess
Victoria, Prince Henry
of Battenberg, Queen
Victoria, Count Mens-
dorff, Princess Henry
of Battenberg, Duchess
of York holding the
Prince Edward, Duke
of York. Seated in front,
Princess Louise, Prince
Waldemar of Prussia
and Prince Alexander of
Battenberg

Queen Alexandra on the Osborne

The Princess of Wales and her children Albert Victor and George and Louise, Victoria and Maud, on board the Royal yacht Osborne, 1880

Alexandra and her family

Prince Albert Victor and Prince George of Wales, H.M.S. Brittania, December, 1877

Alexandra, Princess of Wales, 1864

Alexandra, 1863

Alexandra, 1865

Alexandra and her family. Right: With her daughters

168

Alexandra and Edward VII as Prince and Princess of Wales, Sandringham, 1863

Queen Alexandra and her son who later became King George V

Alexandra when Princess of Wales

Edward VII when Prince of Wales

Princess Alice, June, 1861

Queen Louise of Denmark, Queen Alexandra and Princess Dagmar at Copenhagen

Edward VII and Alexandra
with the King and Queen of
Norway

170   Alexandra

Alexandra

*The King and Queen of Denmark, the King and Queen of Greece and
the Princess of Wales with their children*

*The Queen of Denmark with her grandchildren, the Princesses Louise,
Victoria and Maud*

*Left: Royal gathering at Copenhagen, 1892. Alexandra with the
Tsaritza of all the Russias*

King George V as a boy

The children of Edward VII and Alexandra with (left) the future King George V, 1874

Prince Alfred

Queen Mary and her brothers, 1882

King George VI aged eleven

Prince Leopold

King George VI aged ten

H. M. Queen Alexandra with the Duke of Clarence, 1882

King George V on his honey-moon, 1893

Above: H.M. Queen Mary with her doll, 1870, as a little girl of five, and (left) with her mother, the Duchess of Teck, and her brothers, 1872

H.M. King George V

H.M. Queen Mary with her mother

The Duchess of Teck

H.M. Queen Mary when Princess of Teck, 1885

H.M. Queen Mary as a little girl. The Royal Family group shows the late King George V, H.M. Queen Mary and their children, the Princess Royal, Prince John, Prince George, Prince Edward, Prince Albert and Prince Henry. (Right) H.M. Queen Mary and her brothers with their mother, 1872

H.M. Queen Mary with the Princess Royal

Their Majesties the late King George V and Queen Mary

H.M. Queen Mary, 1910

A portrait of H. M. Queen Mary, when Duchess of York, taken at Sandringham

The Prince of Wales and Prince Albert

Prince Albert

The Princess Royal and her brothers

The Princess Royal and her brothers, the
Prince of Wales and the Duke of York,
1901

H. M. King George VI aged six

Four Generations: T.M. Queen Victoria, King Edward VII,
King George V at the christening of the Prince of Wales,
White Lodge, 1894

Queen Alexandra with her sister

Balmoral, 1910

Alexandra in a sculptor's atelier

Right: Their Majesties King Edward VII and
Queen Alexandra, 1905

*H R H. Princess Eliza-
beth with H.R.H.
Prince Charles of
Edinburgh, 1949*

*The Duchess of Teck
with her daughter,
Mary, 1870*

*H.M. the Queen, then
Duchess of York, with
H.R.H. Princess Eliza-
beth, May, 1926*

*H.M. Queen Victoria
with Princess Beatrice,
1860*

*H.R.H. Princess Eliza-
beth with Princess
Anne, 1950*

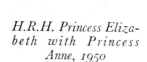

*H.M. Queen Alexandra
with the Princess
Royal, 1868*

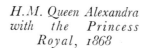

H.M. Queen Elizabeth when Lady Elizabeth Bowes-Lyon, with her brother and dancing teacher, Glamis Castle, 1909

Their Majesties and the Princesses, December, 1936

Left and right: Princess Margaret, June, 1940

Below: Princess Elizabeth, aged four, with her grandmother

Princess Margaret, March 3rd, 1939

Royal Family group, Windsor, April, 1942

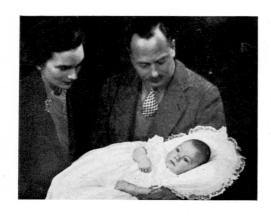

Left: T.R.H. the Duke and Duchess of Gloucester with Prince William

Right: H.R.H the Duchess of Gloucester

Prince Richard and Prince William return from Australia, and (below) Prince William

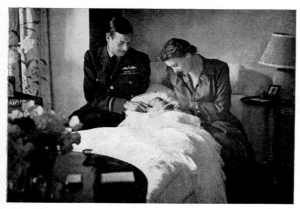

H.R.H. the late Duke of Kent and the Duchess of Kent with Prince Michael, 1942

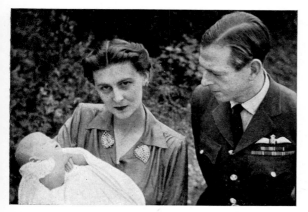

Prince Michael, aged two months, with his parents

Prince Michael and Princess Alexandra with their father

Right above: In the study at The Coppins, Iver, Buckinghamshire

Right: In the Rue de la Paix, Paris. Below: Portraits by Cecil Beaton

H.R.H. the Duke of Windsor

H.R.H. the Princess Royal, the Countess of Harewood

H.R.H. the Duke of Gloucester

The Royal Family during the years of war

Her Majesty the Queen with T.R.H. Princess Elizabeth and Princess Margaret, Buckingham Palace

Above top: Princess Margaret attends her first function. The Princesses on the footplate of the Royal train, South Africa, 1947. Her Majesty the Queen

The Duke and Duchess of Kent in the Bahamas

On the bridge of the
Queen Elizabeth

The Princesses on a South African beach, 1948

Princess Margaret at Anacapri, 1949

The Royal yacht Britannia, *Cowes*

Princess Margaret at Anacapri

H.R.H. the Duchess of
Gloucester

The Queen and Princess Margaret drive to
the Trooping the Colour

H.R.H. the Duchess of
Kent

Queen Alexandra drives in her carriage

Queen Mary drives in her carriage

George VI

The King as a boy

The Princess Royal

H.M. the King. Right: The Duke of Edinburgh

King George V

H.M. the King

H.R.H. the Duke of Kent

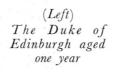

(Left)
The Duke of Edinburgh aged one year

(Lower left)
Princess Elizabeth

(Bottom left)
The Duke of Edinburgh

(Right)
H.R.H. the Duke of Edinburgh joins his ship H . M . S . Chequers as First Lieu-tenant at Malta

(Right below)
The Duke of Edinburgh as a schoolboy

T.R.H. Princess Elizabeth and the Duke of Edinburgh on the christening day of their daughter Princess Anne, 1950

H.R.H. Princess Elizabeth with her two children

Below left: Prince Charles, aged two, with his mother in the grounds of Clarence House

Below: H.R.H. the Duke of Edinburgh

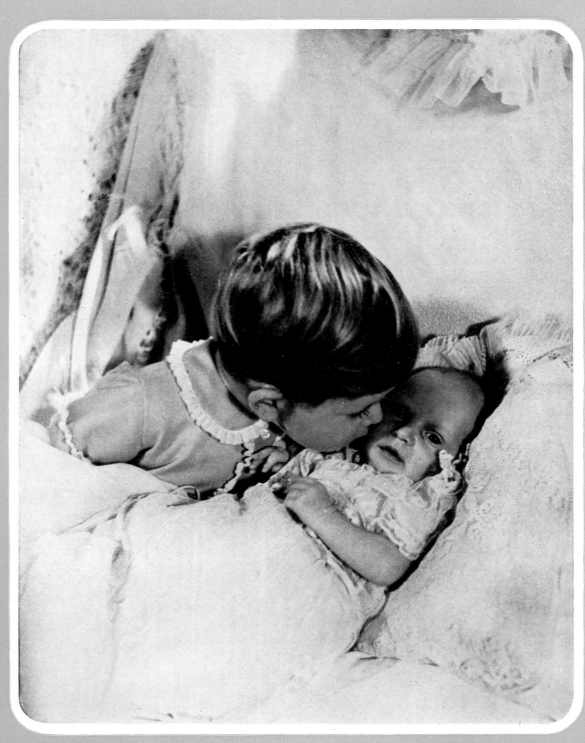

 *Prince Charles and his sister Princess Anne*